LITERARY   INTEREST

LITERARY INTEREST

The Limits of Anti-Formalism

Steven Knapp

Harvard University Press
Cambridge, Massachusetts
London, England
1993

Copyright © 1993 by the President and Fellows of Harvard College
All rights reserved
Printed in the United States of America
10 9 8 7 6 5 4 3 2 1

This book is printed on acid-free paper, and its binding materials have been chosen for strength and durability.

Library of Congress Cataloging-in-Publication Data

Knapp, Steven, 1951-
Literary interest : the limits of anti-formalism / Steven Knapp.
p.   cm.
Includes bibliographical references (p.   ) and index.
ISBN 0-674-53651-7 (acid-free paper)
1. Criticism.   2. Formalism (Literary analysis)   3. Narration
(Rhetoric)   I. Title.
PN98.F6K63   1993
801'.95—dc20
92-44369
CIP

For Diane

Contents

Acknowledgments

This book grows out of a small set of rather obsessive questions with which, for some two decades, I have annoyed anyone who would listen. The people I ought to thank are consequently too numerous to list or even remember; they include, for instance, a very large number of students who have come to my classes hoping to learn something about literature but have found themselves forced instead to worry about the point of it. Several friends and colleagues have been especially (and repeatedly) patient: Paul Alpers, Philip Clayton, Frances Ferguson, Catherine Gallagher, Stephen Greenblatt, Neil Hertz, Jeffrey Knapp, Walter Michaels, Ralph Rader, Anita Sokolsky, and Bernard Williams. And my argument has been shaped (though not always in a way they would have wanted) by many others, some of whom have probably forgotten a discussion or a remark that, to me, was crucial; they include M. H. Abrams, Charles Altieri, Howard Bloch, Stephen Booth, John Coolidge, Jonathan Culler, Richard Feingold, Margaret Ferguson, Philip Fisher, Stanley Fish, Michael Fried, Joseph Graham, Dorothy Hale, Geoffrey Hartman, E. D. Hirsch, Robert Post, Christopher Pye, John Reichert, Michael Rogin, Elaine Scarry, and Randolph Starn. I am grateful to the University of California at Berkeley for a Humanities Research Fellowship that enabled me to begin pursuing this project in earnest during a leave in 1986–87, and to Williams College for the hospitality that let me spend the spring of that year as a visiting scholar in an ideal sabbatical setting. I am also grateful to Bar-

bara Johnson for an invitation to speak at the Center for Literary and Cultural Studies in Cambridge, Massachusetts, where I delivered what later became a large portion of Chapter 3. For practical help of various kinds, finally, I wish to thank Donna Kaiser, Kevin Wertheim, and, once again, Jeffrey Knapp.

Introduction

Western literary theory since Plato has recurrently sought to determine what, if anything, makes literary discourse special. Does its uniqueness lie, as Plato's Socrates argued, in its peculiar (and, in Socrates' view, essentially perverse) distance from what it claims to represent? Or is it distinguished, as Aristotle suggested, mainly by its possession of a unique subject matter, the probable forms of human action? Should we turn instead, as various Romantic theorists did, to an analysis of the mental faculties responsible for the production of what we take to be characteristically literary effects? Or should we follow the lead of those twentieth-century theorists who have attempted to locate the uniqueness of the literary in peculiar features of literary language or, more exactly, in the allegedly special nature of literary semantics?

Recently the difficulty of arriving at any widely persuasive criteria for distinguishing literary from other kinds of discourse has helped to foster a growing agreement, among literary critics and theorists, that literature's uniqueness is an illusion. I say "helped" to foster that agreement, because the denial of any essential difference between literary and non-literary discourse is not simply a result of definitional or taxonomical difficulties. At least equally important has been the claim that accounts of literature's special status have reflected the institutional and political aims of those whose power has depended on the cultural prestige of one or another body of "privileged" texts. Thus it is frequently argued, for instance, that the distinctions between literary and non-literary discourse drawn earlier in this century by the New Critics and other "formalists" were designed, in narrow institutional terms, to encourage and justify the astonishing growth of the English Department and its associated publication industry, and in broader political terms, to defend an idealized vision of cultural activity insulated from social conflict.[1] It follows, for proponents of this view, that a denial of literature's uniqueness is an important, or at least a promising, instrument of institutional and political change.

There is, in short, a great deal to be said about the history and political function of the notion of a uniquely literary mode of discourse. Nevertheless, this book goes against the current tendency by focusing primarily on the theoretical status of the notion itself and only in very general terms on the question of what has followed or might follow, in practice, from accepting or rejecting it. And there is another reason why this book is somewhat unusual in the context of current literary debates: it actually ends up *defending* the notion of "the literary," though it does so in terms that may prove as dismaying to defenders as to critics of literary formalism in its received versions.

This outcome is rather different from the one I anticipated when I started to work on this subject, shortly after finishing a study that concentrated (unlike this one) on some of the historical antecedents of modern literary formalism.[2] I expected to write a book that would, for better or worse, lend theoretical confirmation to the mounting historical and institutional case against formalism.[3] In some respects, my original expectations have been borne out: much of my argument does involve a critique of what might be called the metaphysical case for the literary—that is, of claims for the cognitive and/or semantic uniqueness of literary language, or for the ontological peculiarity of the actions performed by the author of a literary text. But my analysis of the metaphysical case, instead of explaining away the intuition of an important difference between our relation to representations we call literary and our relation to other kind of representation, turned out to give that intuition what seemed to me a surprisingly cogent logical and psychological basis. I came to see that what could not be defended as an account of literary language could be defended instead as an account of a certain kind of representation that provoked a certain kind of *interest*. Using a formula whose abstract claims will be justified, I hope, by later arguments, I propose to call "literary" any linguistically embodied representation that tends to attract a certain kind of interest to itself; that does so by particularizing the emotive and other values of its referents; and that does *that* by inserting its referents into new "scenarios" inseparable from the particular linguistic and narrative structures of the representation itself.

Stated in this way, even with its admittedly daunting abstractness, the formula is likely to sound familiar enough; it recalls the emphasis on particularity and self-reference in New Critical as well as, more recently, in deconstructive accounts of literary representation. The burden of my argument, consequently, will be to show why such an account of the literary, defensible as I will argue it is, nevertheless fails to yield the various cognitive and ethical/political benefits formalists have claimed for it.

But the difference between my account and that of the New Critics (as well as of their more skeptical heirs) goes beyond our differing assessments of what follows from the uniqueness of literary representation. The easiest way to locate the difference is to note the central importance, in my account, of a range of problems involving various types of actual and imagined *agency,* and especially of the apparent tendency of the literary, noted since Plato, to distort or undermine agency in ways that are variously conceived as involving either an irrational fixation or an unstoppable transference or circulation. In Chapter 1, for instance, I focus on the allegedly paradoxical status of the actions performed by literary authors—specifically, the claim that a literary author's action necessarily gives rise to a work whose content goes beyond the one its author intends it to have. My exploration of this problem is complicated, in a typically literary way, by the fact that my example of alleged authorial "failure" (the notorious subversiveness of Milton's *Paradise Lost*) turns out to involve a failed representation of agency within the poem itself. This sort of recursion—where a problem of agency located, as it were, "outside" the work also shows up inside it—is the kind of effect that turns an interpretive problem into a source of literary interest, that is, an interest in the analogical structures whose particularity and complexity give the work its peculiarly literary status.[4]

The theme of agency has by no means been ignored by earlier defenders of literary uniqueness, but their tendency has been to subordinate it to their overriding interest in questions of meaning or knowledge—or rather, in the most prominent cases, to treat the subordination of agency precisely *as* a uniquely literary form of meaning or knowledge. In simplest terms, then, my focus on the vagaries of literary interest is meant to preserve the earlier "formalist" insight that the literary has something to do with an anomalous transformation of agency, but at the same time to resist the notion that its effect on agency involves any kind of semantic or epistemic necessity (or privilege).

In focusing on the claims of the literary, I have refrained from commenting (except briefly in the last chapter) on a subject of equal importance: the claims of *narrative* as a mode of discourse with epistemological, ontological, and axiological properties absent from other modes. The reason is perhaps obvious: the distinction between narrative and non-narrative and the distinction between the literary and the non-literary don't coincide. Narrative can show up anywhere, just as numerous objects of literary interest are devoid of narrative in the usual sense. Indeed, the claims of narrative have recently been extended beyond the bounds of discourse altogether and have been applied to the structure of human experience and value.[5] In any case, it seems to me worth mentioning at the outset the absence of any attempt, in this book, to investigate such claims; nor do I wish to imply that my remarks (skeptical or otherwise) about specifically literary narrative are readily transferable to the question of narrative in general. On the other hand, there is no reason not to hope that the treatment here of certain persistent problems in our notions of action and identity will suggest some of the lines of inquiry that might be pursued in a similar study of narrative.

1

Authorial Action and the Worlds of *Paradise Lost*

The Romantic Argument

Interest in literary works takes innumerable forms, but in our era the theoretical expression of such interest has shown a remarkably consistent tendency to focus on the issue of authorship. I do not mean *authors,* though research into the lives and habits of particular authors continues to account for a large proportion of the work of literary scholars. On the contrary, what has often provoked the kind of theoretical interest I have in mind has been a felt disparity between what we infer, on the basis of biographical or other kinds of evidence, about the meanings an author is likely to have intended and the psychological effects or ideological implications—indeed, the apparent *meaning*—of a work the author in question has produced. The frequent difficulty of explaining the relation between what seems to be the "content" of a work an author produces and what one takes to have been that author's intentions raises the question of whether producing a literary work really is, in any ordinary sense, an *action* that an author performs. If producing literary works is an action, it seems to be a kind of action in which the relation between the agent's intentions and the actual content of what the agent has (somehow) produced is more than usually complex.

The widely shared perception that to compose a literary work is to perform a peculiarly self-transcending action—that the meaning of the work goes beyond what its author intended—seems to me to provide one of the main intuitions underlying the various forms of literary formalism, old and new. In this and the following chapter, I explore the grounds of this proto-formalist intuition, in preparation for a direct theoretical engagement with the claims of formalism in Chapter 3.

Apart from theoretical treatments of the problem, the status of authorial action has nowhere been called into question more frequently or explicitly than in the tradition of commentary on Milton's *Paradise Lost*. Milton intended, it is often argued, in some sense to justify or defend the ways of God; he intended that his poem embody some version of the traditional argument that the origin of evil lies in the free choices of God's rational creatures and not in divine malice or inadvertency. But the actual "meaning" of his poem diverges from what he intended. Whatever Milton wanted to say, the poem itself says that God, not Adam or Eve or Satan, is the source of the world's ills.

My aim in this opening chapter is threefold. In the first place, I want to devise, and to a certain extent defend, a version of what I will call the Romantic Argument, that is, an argument positing a massive disparity between what Milton wanted to do and what he in fact did when he wrote *Paradise Lost*. The Romantic Argument, as I will develop it, will involve a philosophical critique of Milton's account of human agency. Second, I will explore the implications, for literary interpretation generally, of the sort of authorial failure that, if the Romantic Argument is right, Milton's epic can be said to represent. Third, I will suggest that these interpretive and theoretical outcomes leave a certain kind of interest in the problem of Milton's agency unaccounted for. I should emphasize at the outset that my treatment of Milton (and, in the next chapter, of Keats) is not primarily intended as a contribution to current scholarship on Milton (or Keats) but as a preliminary exploration of broader issues whose full theoretical import will emerge in subsequent chapters.

There are several ways of construing the claim that Milton, when he wrote *Paradise Lost,* actually did something other than what he intended to do. It might be construed, for example, as the psychological claim that Milton *unconsciously* intended to undermine his own argument. At least this is one way to understand the most famous instance of what has come to be known as the "Satanic" or "Romantic" reading of *Paradise Lost:* Blake's suggestion that Milton was "of the Devil's party without knowing it."[1] Intriguing as it is and important as it has been historically, this version of the claim is not, however, the one I will address here. For if there is such a thing as an unconscious intention, the Blakean claim does not by itself amount to the theoretically interesting assertion that the content of the poem is not the content Milton gave it; it merely asserts that the poem's subversive meaning is the one Milton in fact (though unconsciously) intended. It leaves no gap, in other words, between intention and content. (On the other hand, Blake's point may not be psychological at all. If the notion of an unconscious intention is incoherent or is only anachronistically attributed to Blake, then Blake's claim may belong instead in one or another of the categories considered below.)

A second version of the Romantic Argument might be called the *rhetorical* version. In this account, Milton's God is simply too unattractive to win an intelligent reader's sympathy. As A. J. A. Waldock puts it, "God, as Milton was able to imagine him, can hardly utter twelve consecutive lines without antagonizing us."[2] This time there is indeed a gap, but not quite between intention and content. The poem's content remains the content Milton intended, even though the poem's *effects* on its readers are not the effects he hoped for and presumably expected. Now a poem's effects on its readers are undeniably central to its role in literary and cultural history. But a disparity between intention and effect is a fate to which all actions are potentially subject. Only if such a disparity is taken to be a *necessary* feature of certain actions does it become theoretically and not just historically or sociologically interesting.

Related to the possibility of a disparity between intention and effect is a disparity between what a text means and what it *exemplifies*. On some accounts, Milton intended to say, and succeeded in saying, that the Fall resulted in part from the relative intellectual deficiency of Eve, who ought to have deferred more consistently to the rational superiority of her husband.[3] But he did not *intend* the poem to exemplify what may seem to us (but would not have seemed to him) an androcentric bias. The fact that it does so, assuming that it does, is, like its psychological effect on its readers, an extremely important fact about *Paradise Lost*. But to exemplify something is not necessarily to *mean* it. If I tell a lie, I am exemplifying dishonesty, but the content of my utterance does not in any plausible sense include my dishonesty. For if it did (to adapt a famous paradox), it wouldn't be a lie, or at least the lie wouldn't work, since I would be telling my audience that I was lying. Similarly, a text can only exemplify an ideological bias if it does not include, as part of its own content, a confession that its truth claims are merely the expression of an ideological bias. This third version of the Romantic Argument—the positing of a disparity between intention and exemplification—is thus historically important but, once again, theoretically not very interesting.

A fourth way to understand the Romantic Argument might be to see it as the (theoretically very interesting) *semantic* claim that the text of *Paradise Lost* necessarily has a different meaning from the one Milton intended, since the structure of language guarantees that meaning always exceeds or departs from authorial intention. I have argued elsewhere against the conception of linguistic meaning this claim would require,[4] and I will not pause to repeat the argument here. If, however, some version of an anti-intentionalist account of meaning were correct, then the notion of authorial action would indeed be problematic in other ways than the ones I will explore.

My focus in what follows will be on what I take to be a fifth way of construing the claim that the content of *Paradise Lost* is not what Milton intended it to be. This version of the Romantic Argument advances the *logical,* or perhaps *metaphysical,* claim that the imagined "world" of Milton's poem is not the world Milton intended to "project."[5] Milton intended to project a world in which Christian theism, as he understood it, was true; in fact, however, the world he actually succeeded in projecting was a world in which essential features of his theism revealed themselves to be false. Something like this view is perhaps suggested by Shelley's remark that "Milton's poem contains within itself a philosophical refutation of that system, of which, by a strange and natural antithesis, it has been a chief popular support."[6] The context of Shelley's statement indicates, however, that he thought of Milton as having secretly intended this result.[7] Only in the twentieth century—above all, in the work of William Empson—does one encounter unambiguous statements of the view that what Empson calls "the logic of his story" undermines Milton's defense of God despite his intentions to the contrary.[8] But my aim in exploring the implications of Shelley's remark is not in any case historical; I will not attempt to establish that any previous interpreter of Milton has held the Romantic position in quite the form I will be considering. My intention is not to describe the forms the argument has taken but to explore what seems to me the most interesting form the argument can take, at least insofar as it bears on the larger problem of authorial action.

The Intended "World"

The argument I will partly invent and partly explore begins like this. In writing *Paradise Lost,* Milton intended to do a number of things, but one of the things he intended to do was to cause his readers to imagine that certain things were the case; that is, he intended his readers to imagine certain states of affairs. Taken together, the various states of affairs Milton wanted his poem to indicate or imply can be called the poem's "world." In addition to intending that his readers imagine certain states of affairs, Milton also intended those imagined states of affairs to be connected to each other in ways that would sustain certain logical inferences from one to another.[9] He intended his reader to imagine states of affairs whose interconnections would be tight enough, for example, to sustain an inference from Eve's speaking to Eve's having a mouth; or from Adam's standing to Adam's being in contact with the ground; or, to take a more interesting case, from God's being God to God's being just, and therefore from God's punishing Adam and Eve to their being *justly* punished, and therefore, finally, to Adam and Eve's being genuinely culpable, genuinely responsible for their crime. The Romantic Arguer then asks if such inferences—at least some of the more interesting and crucial ones—can be sustained, regardless of whether Milton himself (owing to theological tradition, Ramistic training, or personal error) had reason to think they could. For if they *cannot* be sustained, then the poem's world turns out to have a very different content from the one Milton intended to give it. And in that case, it looks as if the determination of what action an author has performed can depend not on the author's intentions but on the outcome of a philosophical inquiry into the structure of the "world" that author has "projected."

Saying that Milton intended his readers to imagine a "world" may give rise, however, to more than one kind of misunderstanding. First, someone might plausibly suppose that the Romantic Arguer considers the projection of a world to have been the only action Milton was performing when he wrote *Paradise Lost.* In fact, however, the poem is full of rhetorical devices—similes, apostrophes, allusions, puns, prolepses, and so on—whose aim and effect are difficult to assimilate to the action of projecting a world. To say that Milton projected an imagined world is not to imply that every aspect of the poem was subordinated to this particular act, as it might have been had Milton been writing a (certain kind of) realistic novel. (Nevertheless, it could turn out that the Romantic Argument has depended from the start on an exaggeration of the poem's novelistic character and hence of the significance of its novelistic "failures.")

A second plausible misapprehension might be that the kind of world at issue here is identical to what metaphysicians call a "possible world." But, as Nicholas Wolterstorff has pointed out, the worlds projected by works of art lack the *completeness* typically involved in the notion of a possible world. A projected world is said to be "complete" or "maximally comprehensive" if, for every state of affairs, the world in question either requires that state of affairs or prohibits it—which amounts to the same thing as saying that every statement about the things in that world is either true or false. For example, if "Lady Macbeth" were the name of an existing person, then in any possible world in which Lady Macbeth existed, she would have given birth to some definite number of children; the statement that she had given birth to three children would thus be either true or false in each of these worlds. In other words, every possible world in which she existed would either require or prohibit the state of affairs that is *Lady Macbeth's having given birth to exactly two children.* But this state of affairs, according to Wolterstorff, is neither required nor prohibited by the world of Shakespeare's play, where *no* definite number of children is assigned to the character named "Lady Macbeth."[10]

Some philosophers would deny, however, that even the *actual* world (which is itself a possible world if any world is) really is maximally comprehensive in Wolterstorff's sense. Even in the actual world, some would argue, there are states of affairs that are neither required nor prohibited, statements that are neither true nor false.[11] In that case, the point about Lady Macbeth can be put in metaphysically neutral terms by saying that the question of how many children she has, or might be imagined as having, plays no role in the extrapolations performed by (most?) interpreters. But there is another reason, for my purposes more important anyway, why imaginary worlds are unlike possible ones: the states of affairs they contain are frequently *im*possible. I will be asking shortly in what sense the world of *Paradise Lost* might be said to contain impossibilities that radically undermine Milton's intentions. But it seems clear that Milton intentionally included at least some impossible states of affairs—for instance, Satan's conversing with various personified abstractions—in the world he intentionally projected.[12] Wherever such impossibilities occur, connections between the poem's imagined states of affairs necessarily break down. While it follows from Eve's speaking (a possible state of affairs) that Eve has a mouth, it is unclear what if anything is supposed to follow about the nature of Chaos from the fact that Chaos at one point actually addresses Satan "With faltering speech and visage incomposed."[13]

Such incoherences, however, are marginal to the poem's central concerns; and in any case, the fact that they are *intended* means that they can't be used to generate a disparity between Milton's intention and the poem's content. To test the Romantic thesis that the world of *Paradise Lost* is importantly different from the one Milton intended to project, we will need to identify states of affairs whose impossibility, if established, would have both unintended and massive consequences for the way we take the poem's world to be structured. The most promising candidates for such a role are already suggested by the history of Milton criticism: they are states of affairs involving controversial aspects of Milton's theism or, more exactly, of the relation between Milton's theism and his representation of human agency.

God, Freedom, and the Logic of Human Agency

Imagine, then, two critics: a convinced "Miltonist," who insists indignantly that Milton did exactly what he intended, and a "Romantic," who relishes the prospect of a sublime, or, if need be, merely a grotesque disparity between the world Milton intended to project and the one he actually projected. We will assume that both critics arrive at the same interpretation of Milton's intentions. They agree that he intended, among other things, to project a world in which God's existing and God's being perfectly just would count as both possible and actual states of affairs. As it happens, the world Milton wanted to project seems to have resembled what he took to be the actual world, since he apparently believed that God actually existed and was actually perfectly just. But even the Miltonist acknowledges that this information about Milton is irrelevant to the content of his intention: he could have been, say, an agnostic and still have tried to project an imaginary world in which Christian theism (that is, roughly the version of Christian theism spelled out in Milton's *Christian Doctrine*) would count as true.[14] In that case, the world he intended to project might still have seemed to him a *possible* state of affairs, though its difference from what he took to be the actual world might have made him less inclined to bother projecting it. Consequently, both parties can agree to ignore the question of whether Milton actually believed in Christian theism, as well as the more difficult question of whether some version of Christian theism is actually true.

Nevertheless, they disagree sharply, and the question over which they disagree is whether the world Milton intended to project—a world in which his version of Christian theism would count as true—is even possible. The Romantic critic maintains that it is not. On what grounds might she maintain this? In what follows I will identify three features of the theism presented in *Paradise Lost* that, if successfully attacked by the Romantic critic, would support a denial not just of the doctrine but of the very coherence of a world in which that doctrine was (putatively) true. All three involve aspects of Milton's defense of God against the charge that he is the author of evil and therefore not really God at all.

First, there is the repeated claim that divine foreknowledge is compatible with human freedom. As God puts it in Book III,

> If I foreknew,
> Foreknowledge had no influence on their fault,
> Which had no less proved certain unforeknown.
> (117–119)

Or as Milton himself puts it in his *Christian Doctrine,* "Though future events will certainly happen, because divine foreknowledge cannot be mistaken, they will not happen by necessity, because foreknowledge, since it exists only in the mind of the foreknower, has no effect on its object."[15] The philosophical question raised by Milton's claim is whether it in fact makes sense to suppose that someone can have infallible knowledge of what an agent will do unless the act in question is necessarily bound to occur; or, conversely, whether an agent's acting freely does not preclude the possibility of anyone's knowing infallibly what the agent will do.

Recently, and perhaps surprisingly, Milton's views on the relation between freedom and foreknowledge have been recalled and criticized by a distinguished philosopher (Anthony Kenny) engaged in the currently widening debate over the logical coherence of theism. Without mentioning Milton, another distinguished philosopher (Alvin Plantinga) has vigorously defended what looks to a lay reader like essentially the same position as Milton's.[16] The current state of the debate leaves open the possibility that, even if Milton's position cannot be defended in the characteristically blunt terms in which he presented it, there may be ways of saving it, perhaps by imposing certain logical restrictions on the sense in which divine foreknowledge can be held to be infallible.

The second issue goes more directly to the heart of the traditional "problem of evil." Suppose we grant that God's foreknowledge is compatible with the freedom his creatures must have if they are to count as responsible for their own evil actions. Why in that case did God create beings he knew would fall? Since he knew what all his creatures would do before he created them, why did he not create only those rational creatures he knew would (freely) obey? If it was possible for him to do so, but he chose not to, then he knowingly permitted evils he could have prevented without in the least diminishing his creatures' freedom. This is the version of the problem of evil that prompted Alvin Plantinga to devise his extraordinary notion of "transworld depravity."[17] According to Plantinga, a critic of the traditional free will defense of theism has to reckon with the possibility that God was metaphysically prohibited from creating a world containing genuinely free agents who would never act wrongly. This would be true if God knew that every possible free creature happened to suffer from transworld depravity—in other words, if God knew that every free creature it was possible for him to create would freely perform some wrong action in every possible world in which that creature existed and which it was possible for God to "actualize." Since, in Milton's world, at least some free creatures—the good angels—apparently lack transworld depravity, the Miltonist would have to adjust Plantinga's basic argument in some way. She might argue, for instance, that (possibly) Milton's God could not have actualized a world containing *as many* good acts as the world he in fact actualized without creating some persons who would sometimes act wrongly. Or she might observe that some kinds of goodness—say, the goodness of a good angel's refusing to join the bad angels—could not have occurred unless certain evils existed first.

The fate of Plantinga's ingenious version of the free will defense is not yet decided. A bibliography in a recent collection of essays on Plantinga's work lists forty-seven items challenging or defending this or other aspects of his treatment of the problem of evil.[18] But it is far from clear in any case how closely the coherence of the world Milton intended to project should be tied to the outcome of Plantinga's kind of logical inquiry. Plantinga's approach depends on the assumption that God created free creatures because he valued their free obedience; it is possible, Plantinga then argues, that a world containing evil was the only world in which such creatures could occur. And certainly Milton's God prefers free obedience to forced submission:

> Not free, what proof could they have given sincere
> Of true allegiance, constant faith or love,
> Where only what they needs must do, appeared,
> Not what they would? What praise could they receive?
> (III.103–106)

But it is uncertain whether he creates free agents solely or primarily *for the sake of* their free obedience. It is at least conceivable that Milton's God creates them for the sake of the entire process of Fall and Redemption outlined in Book III and later somewhat ambiguously celebrated in Adam's controversial lines:

> O goodness infinite, goodness immense!
> That all this good of evil shall produce,
> And evil turn to good; more wonderful
> Than that which by creation first brought forth
> Light out of darkness! Full of doubt I stand,
> Whether I should repent me now of sin
> By me done and occasioned, or rejoice
> Much more, that much more good thereof shall spring,
> To God more glory, more good will to men
> From God, and over wrath grace shall abound.
> (XII.469–478)

If the Fall is, in this special sense, "fortunate,"[19] then Milton's version of the free will defense may be unaffected by the problem that occasioned Plantinga's argument (since God would have had good reason, apart from any metaphysical constraints, to create beings he knew would fall). Nor is it clear how, if this possibility is granted, we might go about deciding whether the goodness of redemption was or was not worth the price of evil. For our notions of what it would take to make existence a great enough good to outweigh a certain quantity of evil are too vague.

In any case, Milton luckily refrains from spelling out God's aims in sufficient detail to show whether or not God would need to avail himself of a Plantinga-style defense. As far as I can see, the poem offers no account at all of God's reasons for creating heaven and the angels. We learn only that he made the angels free, but once again this does not imply that he decided to create them in the first place because he valued freely obedient creatures. Given that he wanted them praiseworthy, it made sense for him to make them free, but why did he *want* them, praiseworthy or otherwise? The only reason God mentions for creating the human race—namely, to replace the fallen angels—is not a genuine reason at all but part of a rhetorical slap at Satan, who overestimates the worth of the angels he has ruined:

> But lest his heart exalt him in the harm
> Already done, to have dispeopled heaven,
> My damage fondly deemed, I can repair
> That detriment, if such it be to lose
> Self-lost, and in a moment will create
> Another world, out of one man a race
> Of men innumerable . . .
>   (VII.150–156)

Precisely the triviality and off-handedness of this ostensible explanation—along with the absence of any other announced reason—prevent one from deciding what ultimate good God might be aiming at, and consequently from even attempting to decide whether that good might be attainable without the production of evil side-effects.[20] In short, even without Plantinga's "transworld depravity" or the hypothesis of a fortunate Fall, it seems difficult to exclude the possibility that Milton's God is justified, on the basis of some hidden or even inconceivable greater good, in creating beings he knows will choose evil.

Suppose it turns out, then, that the coherence of the world Milton intended to project is not seriously impugned by these first two objections to the cogency of his free will defense of God. Suppose further that the Romantic critic agrees. She now grants that divine foreknowledge is logically compatible with angelic and human freedom, and that there are insufficient grounds for arguing that Milton's God could have produced a world containing a better balance of good and evil than the world he in fact produced. She can still point to another controversial notion, one to which Milton's version of theism seems irrevocably committed: the notion of free agency as such. For if *this* proves incoherent, then none of the strategies that might be devised to shore up other aspects of Milton's "free will defense" of God's justice will matter. It won't matter, for instance, whether foreknowledge can be proven to be compatible with free agency if free agency itself is impossible. And the Romantic critic sees a further advantage in this third issue: unlike the first two, which suffer from a certain abstractness and are likely to seem remote from most of the poem's characters and incidents, this question has inescapable implications for the entire narrative. After all, a Miltonist who was convinced that divine foreknowledge and free agency were incompatible might simply, if regretfully, jettison the lines referring to divine foreknowledge. This might leave a significant hole in the poem; the Miltonist would have to acknowledge that Milton had not fully succeeded in projecting the world he intended to project. In doing so, however, she would merely be reviving a standard eighteenth-century critical practice; one thinks of Samuel Johnson's readiness to diagnose and recommend the excision of some local absurdity, without seeming to worry that the poem in question might not survive the operation. The Miltonist might be able to treat Milton's lines about divine foreknowledge in the same rather casual way.

On the other hand, if free agency turns out to be a logical tumor, it looks inoperable. The stakes here are of course familiar to every reader of Milton. If one is a determinist, then everything that counts, according to Milton's libertarianism, as a mere temptation that a rational agent is free to resist becomes an irresistible cause of action. Every detail in the account of Adam and Eve's experience in the Garden is transformed if one supposes that the narrative provides a causal explanation of their Fall, instead of merely describing options between which they are genuinely free to choose. If they are not free, then Milton's God, by the logic both he and Milton endorse, cannot justly hold them accountable for their actions. And in that case, all the numerous states of affairs that depend on God's justly holding Adam and Eve accountable are rendered incoherent, or at least deprived of any coherent connection to the rest of the poem's content.

The Romantic critic's enthusiasm for this scenario should not, however, obscure the difficulty of what she has to prove. One way for her to proceed might be to demonstrate that the conception of human agency entailed by libertarianism is *empirically* impossible, given the way human agents are in fact put together; libertarianism would thus resemble, in this respect, the notion that the moon is made of green cheese. It is unlikely, however, that anyone is presently in possession of empirical evidence that firmly rules out the possibility that human beings have free will, assuming that the existence of such evidence is itself even possible. A more promising line of attack might be an argument showing that the libertarian conception of agency is not simply mistaken but incoherent. But how would the Romantic go about proving *that?* I will offer a single strategy, one of several that could be derived from the philosophical literature on free will. Once again, my aim will not be to settle the question of whether Milton's representation of agency is in fact coherent; I will merely indicate a line of inquiry that, if pursued far enough, might justifiably affect our sense of the relation between the world Milton intended to project and the one he in fact projected.

Consider, then, what has to be possible if Adam is to count as a free agent in the sense apparently required by Milton's intentions. It has to be possible for Adam to count as the undetermined origin of his actions; he has to have the ability, in other words, to act without being compelled to do so by any antecedent state of affairs. It is not sufficient that he be *relatively* autonomous—autonomous, that is, only in the sense that his actions, though causally determined by his prior inclinations and beliefs, are nevertheless not compelled by external force or some internal pathology. Such relative autonomy may be sufficient for our ordinary practice of holding people morally responsible for their actions; if so, then free will, in the only sense required by our ordinary practice, is fully compatible with determinism. And in fact, "compatibilism" (the doctrine that determinism and freedom are mutually compatible) has been, at least in British and American philosophy, the dominant account of freedom since Hobbes.[21]

Whatever may be true in *our* world, however, compatibilism is clearly not a coherent option in the world Milton intends to project. The difficulty lies in Milton's (version of) theism. Compatibilism assumes that it makes sense to ascribe moral responsibility to relatively autonomous agents in part because no better candidate is available. But in *Paradise Lost,* any event not caused by a created agent who is autonomous in a more than relative sense must be traced to God, who sets up all the initial conditions that, on determinist assumptions, necessarily eventuate in the actions of his creatures. To say that Adam's disobedience is determined by his prior dispositions is necessarily to say that his disobedience is caused by God, who created those dispositions with full knowledge of what actions they would determine. Nor is Milton's God unaware of the requirement that his rational creatures be free in a thoroughly incompatibilist sense:

> So without least impulse or shadow of fate,
> Or aught by me immutably foreseen,
> They trespass, authors to themselves in all
> Both what they judge and what they choose; for so
> I formed them free, and free they must remain,
> Till they enthrall themselves; I else must change
> Their nature, and revoke the high decree
> Unchangeable, eternal, which ordained
> Their freedom, they themselves ordained their fall.
>   (III.120–128)

Or as Milton elsewhere puts it, in words that could be transferred, with only terminological alterations, to a modern philosophical paper on the subject:

> From the concept of freedom . . . all idea of necessity must be removed. No place must be given even to that shadowy and peripheral idea of necessity based on God's immutability and foreknowledge. If any idea of necessity remains . . . , it either restricts free agents to a single course, or compels them against their will, or assists them when they are willing, or does nothing at all. If it restricts free agents to a single course, this makes man the natural cause of all his actions and therefore of his sins, just as if he were created with an inherent propensity towards committing sins. If it compels free agents against their will, this means that man is subject to the force of another's decree, and is thus the cause of sins only *per accidens,* God being the cause of sin *per se.* If it assists free agents when they are willing, this makes God either the principal or the joint cause of sins. Lastly, if it does nothing at all, no necessity exists.[22]

At the heart of Milton's arguments about freedom lies a simple dilemma: either an act is undetermined by anything but the agent's choice, or something (or someone) other than the agent is responsible for it. To which an anti-libertarian will unhesitatingly respond with a strikingly similar dilemma: either an act is determined by something more than the agent's choice, or it is a sheer accident for which *no one* is responsible. Here, for instance, displaying an impatient rigor reminiscent of Milton's own, is A. J. Ayer:

> We must ask how it is that I come to make my choice. Either it is an accident that I choose to act as I do or it is not. If it is an accident, then it is merely a matter of chance that I did not choose otherwise; and if it is merely a matter of chance that I did not choose otherwise, it is surely irrational to hold me responsible for choosing as I did. But if it is not an accident that I choose to do one thing rather than another, then presumably there is some causal explanation of my choice: and in that case we are led back to determinism.[23]

Actually, Ayer's dilemma leads either to determinism or to a rejection of moral responsibility; it is consistent with both a compatibilist and a skeptical analysis of freedom. But either of these outcomes will satisfy the Romantic critic, who has no interest in providing a coherent justification of moral responsibility but merely wants to show the incoherence of Milton's libertarianism. The disadvantage of Ayer's argument is that it seems question-begging, since it simply assumes that an act not explained by prior states of affairs is inexplicable.[24] It excludes in advance exactly what the libertarian view requires: the possibility of what some philosophers call "immanent" or "agent causation," that is, causal determination of events by an agent whose decision to cause those events is not in turn determined by anything else. According to a prominent defender of this notion of causation, "We have a prerogative which some would attribute only to God: each of us, when we act, is a prime mover unmoved. In doing what we do, we cause certain events to happen, and nothing—or no one—causes us to cause those events to happen."[25]

The fact that it begs the question against agent causation is no doubt a defect in Ayer's argument. But this weakness would seem more damaging if anyone could give a convincing account of how there could be such a thing as agent causation or, more important, how an appeal to this notion really enhances the plausibility of libertarianism. For if the agent, in the moment of free decision, is causally disconnected from his/her prior mental states, then what exactly makes the self that performs the act identical to the self that already existed before the decision occurred? It would seem that the self, in this account, is in an important sense re-created in the moment of decision, so that the "self" responsible for the act is discontinuous with its own history. By appealing to the notion of agent causation, then, libertarianism may indeed escape Ayer's dilemma; the free act no longer seems an accident that simply happens to the agent. But the new alternative seems equally unsettling: it now seems that the agent herself, as she exists in the moment of freedom, is an accident that happens to her own pre-existing self. Nor will it help matters if the libertarian tries to restore some measure of continuity, for instance by allowing the agent's prior desires (Eve's hunger, or her wish to be independent) to contribute causally to her decision without determining it.[26] For as long as anything at all is left up to the agent as she will exist, undetermined, in the moment of decision, what will result from her desires—or from any other states of affairs involving her pre-existing self—remains a matter of chance.[27] It is hard, in short, to see how the self can be anything more than the innocent victim, or else the undeserving beneficiary, of its own free agency. If there is no plausible way to integrate the moment of freedom into the ongoing life of the self, it would seem that freedom has been preserved only at the cost of making ascriptions of responsibility pointless.

And in fact (the Romantic critic goes on), certain moments in *Paradise Lost* give unintended evidence that someone's free agency can only be an accident that befalls her. Consider Adam's remarks on freedom in his debate with Eve over her proposal that they temporarily separate to make their gardening more efficient:

> . . . God left free the will, for what obeys
> Reason, is free, and reason he made right,
> But bid her well beware, and still erect,
> Lest by some fair appearing good surprised
> She dictate false, and misinform the will
> To do what God expressly hath forbid.
> . . . . .
> Firm we subsist, yet possible to swerve,
> Since reason not impossibly may meet
> Some specious object by the foe suborned,
> And fall into deception unaware,
> Not keeping strictest watch, as she was warned.
> (IX.351–356, 359–363)

At first this passage seems to preserve the causal integrity of the self, since the will's freedom entails its direct dependence on the dictates of reason. But this device merely shifts the locus of immanent causation from the will to the faculty of reason, which is itself apparently capable of spontaneous action: faced with a specious object, it may or may not exert the appropriate effort of vigilance. Reason itself, in other words, is strangely endowed with something like its own internal version of free will. Exactly why it should ever fail to exert the requisite energy, given that God has made it "right," is of course unexplained. But even if that supposition is coherent, it seems clear that the rest of the self, including the will, is left at the mercy of reason's spontaneous agency.

The Gnostic Alternative

I am not supposing that this line of attack will leave the Miltonist speechless. One obvious response would be to challenge the notion of personal identity it takes for granted, perhaps by arguing that the self is a substance that persists across psychological discontinuities. Certainly this notion is available in the traditions lying behind Milton's account, though it is crucial to keep in mind that what matters is whether such an account is *in fact* coherent, not whether Milton might have had reason to think it was. Alternatively, the Miltonist might settle for a purely metonymic connection between the ongoing history of the self and the moments of freedom that periodically interrupt that history. The agent alive in the moment of free decision might be the only entity that is literally responsible, but the self that pre-exists and survives the event might count as responsible in some derived or figurative sense, if only because it is unable to *deny* its connection with the acts that interrupt and redirect its history. (Compare Milton's mysterious remarks on God's punishing the serpent: "though brute, *unable to transfer* / The guilt on him who made him instrument / Of mischief" [X.165–167; emphasis added].) Or, more radically, the Miltonist might argue that Milton's libertarianism is intended to count not merely as true but as *incorrigibly* true; despite its apparent unintelligibility, its truth is built into the poem's world in a way that precludes rational assessment.[28]

I find the first two possibilities intriguing, and in fact I will defend a version of the second one (though not directly in relation to Milton) in Chapter 5. Meanwhile, exploring either of these options would take us too far outside the terms of the present debate. As for the third response, in arguing that the poem's libertarianism is to be understood not rationally but fideistically, the Miltonist might be right but would be violating the initial terms of the debate by introducing a new interpretation of Milton's intentions. It might be true that Milton never intended to project a world whose coherence was in principle subject to rational assessment; in that case, however, the Romantic objection would not be false but simply irrelevant.

I conclude, then, for the sake of the present argument, that the Romantic critic has succeeded, at least within the original terms of the debate, in showing that the state of affairs consisting in Adam's justly meriting the wrath of God by an undetermined act of disobedience is impossible. Unlike the local damage inflicted on the poem's world by impossibilities resulting, for instance, from Milton's scientific beliefs, the damage in this case appears to be massive. For, assuming as Milton does that God infallibly knows what is just and never acts unjustly, if it is impossible that God justly blame Adam for his act of disobedience, then it is impossible that God impose the penalties whose operation constitutes the action of Books X through XII. It is equally impossible that God establish the mechanism of redemption announced in Book III. And it is also impossible that God send the archangel Raphael on a mission to warn Adam and thus ensure that he will be fully responsible for the Fall—which is to say that the main action of Books V through VIII has no logical connection to the rest of the poem. And so on.

Each of these impossible events can of course be broken down into smaller components that will permit a coherent construction of local narrative "worlds."[29] For example, even if it is impossible that God send the Son to pass "mortal sentence" on man's transgression (X.34–62), it remains perfectly possible for Adam and Eve to lament the condition in which they now find themselves and thus to undergo the process of reconciliation that concludes the action of Book X. But there is no way to make sense of any connection between their repentance and what professes to be God's partial acceptance of it at the beginning of Book XI, since, once again, it is impossible for God, if he *is* God in Milton's sense, to have held them responsible for their crime in the first place.

This picture of what might be called massive inter-episodic breakdown brings us to the center of this chapter's concerns. For what

exactly does it imply about the status of authorial intention and, consequently, the nature of authorial action? So far the Romantic critic has only shown the impossibility of connecting the poem's episodes in the way Milton intended them to be connected. Why not, then, simply read the poem as a collection of fragments, each of which, taken separately, coherently indicates a state of affairs Milton intended to project? Milton, on this account, has not written an epic with the meaning he intended, but it is not clear that he has therefore succeeded, as the Romantic Argument seems to envision, in writing a *different* epic, with a *different* meaning from the one he intended. By failing to establish the logical interconnections he wanted his episodes to have, Milton has failed to project the large-scale coherent or roughly coherent world he intended to project. Has he for that reason succeeded in projecting a different world, a world that in fact coheres but on different assumptions from the ones he intended? Why might it seem plausible to suppose that authorial failure entails the replacement, and not simply the destruction, of a work's intended content?

What makes it seem plausible to replace and not just abandon the world Milton failed to project is, I suspect, the interpretive necessity of extrapolation, a necessity that would obtain whether or not Milton succeeded in projecting the world he intended. In deciding what belongs to the world of any work, we inevitably fill in the information needed to connect and explain the states of affairs an author has linguistically indicated.[30] If this procedure makes sense in general, why not use it to re-establish connections between episodes whose intended relations have been destroyed by conceptual discoveries the author could not have anticipated? After all, consider how easy it is to supplement *Paradise Lost* with information that will compensate for our (hypothetical) discovery that Milton's libertarianism is incoherent. One can simply add the information, for instance, that the God who announces his plan of redemption in Book III, dispatches Raphael in Book V, is recalled creating our universe in Book VII, and then hands out various penalties in Books X through XII is not really (what Milton means by the term) God. His words, when he identifies himself and explains his actions, mean exactly what Milton intends them to mean, and he says exactly what Milton intends him to say. The trouble is that Milton's God is *lying*—calling himself "God" when he knows he isn't, imposing penalties he knows to be unjust, and so on.[31] On the other hand, perhaps Milton's God is not lying but is simply mistaken:

he believes himself to be omniscient, but we infer from his regrettable confusion about free agency that he is not really omniscient and therefore, once again, not really God. In either of these two cases, the world of the poem ceases to be a world in which Milton's version of Christian theism merely fails to be true and becomes instead a world in which the creator is a lying or deluded Demiurge. It becomes, in other words, a world containing the states of affairs suggested by one or another variation on classical Gnosticism.[32]

The doctrine that turns out to be true in this world need not, however, share the pessimism often imputed to Gnosticism in its ancient forms. Perhaps the malice or error that motivates Milton's creator-demon is, by a providential agency superior to his own, actually in the service of some larger scheme of redemption in which, for instance, the Son rather than the Father, or perhaps the Holy Light invoked in Book III, will turn out to be the true origin and center of the Godhead.

In any event, one or another of these scenarios has of course been the outcome sought all along by the Romantic critic. In fact, an implicit equation of Milton's God and the Gnostic Demiurge is what Empson's reading of Milton is all about. Occasionally the equation becomes explicit—for instance, when Empson connects with Gnosticism his notion that Milton's God will eventually abdicate his throne so that all existence can be united to the One.[33] In the chapter of "final reflections" added to the 1981 edition of his book, Empson goes so far as to treat a variation on this Gnostic scheme as the poem's "main story": "The main story of Milton is that, though God causes much suffering, he takes no pleasure in it; it is merely needed for his high purpose, arrived at before the creation, of evolving a society so perfect that he may allow himself to abdicate into it."[34]

Quite apart, however, from whatever desirability it may have in other respects, the Gnostic solution immediately repairs the inter-episodic breakdown we encountered earlier. For there is nothing impossible or incoherent about a malicious Demiurge merely *claiming* that it makes sense to punish creatures he secretly knows to be innocent. We need only suppose that he has an impressive ability to deceive his creatures, including the angels and perhaps also the narrator, who now turns out, despite Milton's intentions, to be an unreliable one.

The question I wish to pose, then, is this: does it in fact make sense to think of the Romantic or Gnostic alternative to the world Milton intended to project as the world he actually succeeded in projecting?

In one respect, after all, the newly repaired world is closer to Milton's intention than the incoherent one he thought he was projecting. Part of his intention was generic; he intended to project the kind of world that one projects by writing an epic. If the Romantic critic is right, however, the impossibilities produced by the conjunction of Milton's theism and his libertarianism reduce the poem to a tragedy or a series of brief tragedies, arbitrarily linked to various allegorical interludes, chunks of confused theology, and parodies of Homer. The War in Heaven, for instance, cannot be integrated into the narrative either as an explanation of the origin of evil or as a warning to Adam and Eve, since the cogency of the explanation and the rationale of the warning are both destroyed by the incoherence of Milton's criteria of responsibility. If Milton intended to write an epic, and if the poem's status as epic can be saved on Gnostic assumptions, then surely it makes more sense to read *Paradise Lost* as a coherent Gnostic epic than as an arbitrary collection of Christian fragments.

This proposal, if accepted, would have several attractive consequences that even the Miltonist may by now be in a position to appreciate. It would guarantee the success of Milton's fundamental act of projecting a world, even if it did so at the expense of his apologetic aims. It would make the critic's own activity no longer parasitic on Milton's authorial action but essential to its completion. And it would yield a general principle of critical supplementation: when reconstructing the world projected by any authorial action, a critic is not only free to extrapolate by including in the imagined world states of affairs that follow from what the author has indicated, as Lady Macbeth's having given birth presumably follows from her having given suck; a critic is also empowered to imagine additional states of affairs that will enhance the coherence of the world projected by the author, even if the states of affairs thus added are utterly foreign to the author's intentions.

As soon as it suggests this general principle, however, the Gnostic proposal reveals its irrelevance to the issue of Milton's success or failure. For the fact that Milton or any author has failed to project the world he intended to project is altogether irrelevant to the fact that a critic can revise the content of an imagined world by imagining states of affairs that go beyond authorial intention. Once a critic is free to add new states of affairs (instead of merely filling in information entailed by what an author has indicated), why bother to stipulate that such additions must enhance the imagined world's coherence? Or if the value of coherence seems self-explanatory, why restrict the work of critical supplementation to the restoration of large-scale coherences like the ones involved in the Gnostic supposition that Milton's God is lying or ignorant? Early in Book IX, as was mentioned earlier, Eve rather inexplicably suggests that she and Adam temporarily separate; Satan is consequently able, by an extraordinary coincidence, to catch her by herself. Why not add, in the spirit of the Gnostic proposal, that Eve's suggestion was secretly instigated by God? In Book VIII, while Adam continued his conversation with Raphael, Eve went off to tend her flowers (39–47); perhaps God sent a second archangel to hypnotize Eve and give her subliminal instructions to be carried out a week later on the morning Satan would return to the Garden. The possibility of elaborating the poem in this fashion in no way depends on a prior demonstration that Milton's theism is incoherent. The elaborator might just as easily suppose that God's reasons for having Eve hypnotized are entirely benevolent: perhaps he wants to give her obedience a fair test, which it won't receive unless Satan has a chance to tempt her while Adam is elsewhere.

The suggestion that Milton's failure might permit a critic to replace his intended world with a new one is thus mistaken, for at least two reasons. First, as we have just seen, the possibility of supplementing the content of an imagined world is independent of any determination of authorial success or failure; there is nothing in either case to prevent a critic from elaborating an imagined world in any way she wishes. If Milton's projecting a different world from the one he intended means only that it is possible to supplement the world he projected, then the gap between intention and result is trivial; in this sense, every author always automatically succeeds in projecting worlds that differ from the one he/she intended. Second, inventions like my Archangelical Mesmerist could be multiplied endlessly; at what point, if not immediately, would the supplementing critic feel disinclined to suppose that the resulting world was still the world of Milton's *Paradise Lost?* It would seem easier to admit from the start that to supplement a poem with information foreign to its author's intentions is not to elaborate the poem's world but to imagine a different world—indeed, to imagine a different poem—whether or not one retains ingredients from the original poem's world.[35]

The Romantic Argument, then, even if it succeeds in demonstrating the incoherence of Milton's theism, can only show that Milton's world fails to cohere in the way he intended. It cannot show that the world Milton actually projected is, except in this negative sense, a different world from the one he intended to project. It cannot, in other words, produce a theoretically interesting gap between authorial intention and literary content. At best, the Romantic Argument yields a scenario that oddly *resembles* an interesting gap between intention and content. This effect may be peculiar to *Paradise Lost,* an anomalous result of its precarious dependence on the controversial logic of the free will defense of theism. As we have seen, if the philosophical objections to Milton's libertarianism were to prove correct, the damage to the intended world of *Paradise Lost* would be irreparably massive. But so little supplementation would be required to turn Milton's God into a Gnostic Demiurge, and the result—coherence—would be so close to what Milton presumably wanted to achieve, that a critic might be forgiven for succumbing to a certain illusion. The illusion would be that Milton, despite his intentions, succeeded in writing a Gnostic epic. The truth would be that he failed to write an epic.

Interpretation and Interest

If the argument to this point has been right, there is a sense in which a literary work can fail to have the content, and therefore fail even to have the form, that its author intended it to have. (Again I should emphasize that the failure in Milton's case remains hypothetical; my intent has not been actually to endorse the Romantic Argument, or even to treat it as an adequate response to state-of-the-art Milton criticism, which some might say has rendered Empson's style of novelistic criticism obsolete.) Such authorial failure is possible even if there is no plausible sense in which the work can acquire a *new* content in place of the intended one. But, as I remarked at the outset, this outcome does not yet account for an important sense in which one's interest in the problem of Milton's authorial agency can go beyond an interpretive interest in figuring out what action Milton performed or failed to perform, as well as beyond a theoretical interest in Milton's authorial agency as illustrating a general truth about literary meaning.

Simply put, what I have in mind is an interest in the parallel between Milton's own agency and agency as he represents it within the poem. This chapter began, after all, with the question of Milton's rela-

tion to the world he intended to project or, in more traditional terminology, to "create"; is it just an accident that the charge of authorial
failure centers on Milton's depiction of God's relation to the world *he*
created? And is it just an accident that the coherence of God's agency,
as Milton imagines it, turns out to depend on the cogency of Milton's
libertarianism—that is, on the cogency of his picture of the self's relation to its supposedly free actions? Doesn't this complex analogy—
relating Milton's authorship to God's creativity, and each of these in
turn to Adam's and Eve's self-authoring freedom ("authors to themselves in all / Both what they judge and what they choose")—doesn't
all this demand explicit treatment as an essential part of the theoretical
problem I have been addressing?

But what role exactly should the analogy play? Are the three problems of agency treated in this chapter in fact analogous in ways that
should alter its conclusions? The unavoidable answer, I think, is that
they are not. For the particular source of (alleged) failure or incoherence relevant to each problem is not in any clear sense transferable to
the other two. Thus the (alleged) incoherence of the libertarian account
of human freedom makes Milton's particular version of theism also
incoherent, but not quite for the same reason: the collapse of *human*
freedom doesn't show God to be unfree but either ignorant or unjust.
Similarly, the (alleged) failure of Milton's theism amounts to the
failure of his own authorial action, but only for the contingent reason
that he intended, as it happens, to project a world in which his theism
would count as true; he might have intended something else and succeeded in doing what he intended. In short, the arguments we have
considered count, if valid, against the success of Milton's particular act;
but Milton's failure doesn't show that authors have to fail.

If it doesn't affect the theoretical outcome, is an analogy among the
various cases of agency at least part of the poem's intended meaning, so
that it can be said to have a thematic or interpretive importance even if
it lacks a theoretical one? There is no reason in principle why Milton
might not have intended to project an analogy between, say, divine
and poetic creativity. Given the references to Creation in his epic invo-
cations, critics have typically assumed that suggesting such analogies
was, in fact, part of his intention. But presumably he didn't intend
that the failure of his own agency would turn out, ironically, to lie in a
failure precisely of his account of agency. For he did not, presumably,
intend either failure. And even if he intended to thematize his own

authorial agency and to invite us to relate it somehow to God's agency or Adam's, it seems at best unlikely that he would have intended to present the problem of authorial agency in anything like the form in which that problem comes down to us from Romantic and post-Romantic aesthetics.

In general, an interest in analogies between poets and their poems, or poets and readers, or readers and poems is hard to account for in either theoretical or interpretive terms. But my claim is not that a non-interpretive and non-theoretical interest in analogies is for that reason anomalous or mistaken. On the contrary, it is precisely for this kind of interest that I propose to reserve the adjective "literary." The argument of this chapter has not been against the legitimacy of literary interest but only against the notion that the source of such interest lies in the peculiar ontology of a literary work's content.

2

Negative Capability

Passive Agency

At the end of the previous chapter I mentioned the difficulty of exploring Milton's picture of God or his libertarian conception of moral "self-authorship" without being reminded of Milton's own authorial agency. But in taking on the role of an epic poet, Milton necessarily refrains from depicting his own agency in libertarian terms; nor does he claim to possess anything like the freedom he imputes to God. Not only is poetic agency, as Milton describes it, not free; it isn't even voluntary, at least when working properly. Thus the poet hopes that he and his poem will achieve "heroic name," but they won't do so "if all be mine, / Not hers who brings it nightly to my ear" (*Paradise Lost,* IX.44–47). He actively persists despite his blindness, but his only persistent *action* is to wander in search of an agency outside himself:

> Yet not the more
> Cease I to wander where the Muses haunt
> Clear spring, or shady grove, or sunny hill,
> Smit with the love of sacred song . . .
> (III.26–29)

And if the poet's thoughts are at one point said to be voluntary—"thoughts, that voluntary move / Harmonious numbers" (III.38–39)—the point of calling them voluntary is to capture the impression that, despite their remaining in some sense *his* thoughts, they proceed independently of his deliberate direction. Poetic agency, as such passages describe it, seems rather distant from rational will or vigilant reason and rather closer, for instance, to the wandering inadvertency of Eve. Or perhaps to Satan when he looks at Eve and then sees his own agency as having wandered away from will and purpose:

> Thoughts, whither have ye led me, with what sweet
> Compulsion thus transported to forget
> What hither brought us . . .
>   (IX.473–475)

It is unclear, in short, whether Milton's picture of authorial action fits the theory of agency on which, I argued, he hinged the very coherence of the world his poem projected.

In the context of epic, of course, the claim to surrender one's own agency to a higher power is at the same time a conventional act of self-assertion: to profess reliance on the Muse is also to proclaim one's fitness to soar. Even when combined, as in Milton's case, with a religious ideal of patience, it is plainly meant to be taken with a grain of learned salt. Nevertheless, I propose in this chapter to take seriously the possibility that such gestures of self-abnegation point to a genuine feature of literary action, even if the feature in question will turn out to lack the metaphysical or moral importance sometimes imputed to it. As I will argue, the peculiar passivity of authorial agency has nothing to do either with the production of a special non-intentional meaning (a meaning the tale has apart from the one given by the teller) or with a moral transcendence of selfhood. Seeing what it *does* involve will enable us to isolate further a peculiar kind of interest that was introduced in the previous chapter and will be explored at length in the next one.

Keatsian Speculation

Certainly the most suggestive name for the paradoxical kind of agency I have in mind is the phrase that provides the title of this chapter. It comes from an early letter by John Keats, who seems to have used it only on that occasion. The phrase itself is of course extremely famous (even occurring, to my knowledge, in at least one movie by Woody Allen), but the context in which it first occurred is worth recovering. The train of thought that leads up to it apparently begins when Keats, writing to his brothers George and Tom (21, 27 [?] December 1817), explains his dissatisfaction with Benjamin West's painting *Death on the Pale Horse:*

> It is a wonderful picture, when West's age is considered; But there is nothing to be intense upon; no women one feels mad to kiss; no face swelling into reality. The excellence of every Art is its intensity, capable of making all disagreeables evaporate, from their being in close relationship with Beauty & Truth—Examine King Lear & you will find this exemplified throughout; but in this picture we have unpleasantness without any momentous depth of speculation excited, in which to bury its repulsiveness.[1]

I will return later to the notion of burying repulsiveness in a depth of speculation. What matters for now is the way this account of readerly speculation leads to a parallel account of authorial hesitation or suspension. The passage just quoted is followed by a series of apparently unrelated remarks on various activities and acquaintances; eventually Keats returns to Shakespeare by way of reporting a "disquisition" he had with his friend Dilke "on various subjects":

> Several things dovetailed in my mind, & at once it struck me, what quality went to form a Man of Achievement especially in Literature & which Shakespeare possessed so enormously—I mean *Negative Capability,* that is when man is capable of being in uncertainties, Mysteries, doubts, without any irritable reaching after fact & reason—Coleridge, for instance, would let go by a fine isolated verisimilitude caught from the Penetralium of mystery, from being incapable of remaining content with half knowledge. This pursued through Volumes would perhaps take us no further than this, that with a great poet the sense of Beauty overcomes every other consideration, or rather obliterates all consideration. (*Letters,* I, 193)

It is easy to see Keats's notion of negative capability as paralleling his explicitly ethical remarks, on other occasions, on what he calls "disinterestedness." But the parallel is in fact misleading, at least if it leads one to think that negative capability itself is implicitly an ethical notion.[2] In the first place, when Keats writes his fullest account of ethical disinterestedness, he neglects even to mention the issue of *aesthetic* excellence that concerns him in the letter on negative capability:

> Very few men have ever arrived at a complete disinterestedness of Mind: very few have been influenced by a pure desire of the benefit

of others . . . I have no doubt that thousands of people never heard
of have had hearts comp[l]etely disinterested: I can remember but
two—Socrates and Jesus—What I heard a little time ago, Taylor
observe with respect to Socrates, may be said of Jesus—That he was
so great a man that though he transmitted no writing of his own to
posterity, we have his Mind and his sayings and his greatness handed
to us by others. (*Letters,* II, 79–80)

The surprising absence here (if one supposes that disinterestedness is
connected to negative capability) is that of Shakespeare. But in fact
literary excellence in general is excluded from Keats's ethical ideal; the
disinterested include thousands of people "never heard of," plus Socrates and Jesus—neither of whom, notoriously, was a writer. When
Keats *does* turn, a few sentences later, to the question of poetry, he
explicitly contrasts an aesthetic appreciation of error with a philosophical pursuit of truth:

Though a quarrel in the streets is a thing to be hated, the energies
displayed in it are fine; the commonest Man shows a grace in his
quarrel—By a superior being our reasoning[s] may take the same
tone—though erroneous they may be fine—This is the very thing in
which consists poetry; and if so it is not so fine a thing as
philosophy—For the same reason that an eagle is not so fine a thing
as a truth. (*Letters,* II, 80–81)

Prooftexting from Keats's letters is, however, an unreliable method
of pinning down his aesthetic; given the immense production of poems
and letters between the negative capability letter and the letter on disinterestedness, and considering that Keats was in no sense a systematic
thinker, there is no way to be certain, solely on the basis of these letters, that he didn't simply change his mind. It could be the case, in
other words, that when Keats wrote "disinterestedness" he still meant
the same ideal he had meant when he wrote "negative capability," but
that, in the meantime, he had lost his faith that poetry was a plausible
medium in which to achieve it.

Fortunately we don't have to rely on such doctrinal statements in
order to get at what is involved in negative capability—and thus to see
why an ethical interpretation of it has to be mistaken. Instead, we can
attend to the way the connection Keats draws, in the negative capability letter, between readerly speculation and authorial suspension
works itself out, as it were, "in practice." Consider, to begin with, the

following episode. On 3 February 1820 Keats suffered a lung hemor-
rhage and coughed up the bright red blood that convinced him his
illness was terminal. "I know the colour of that blood," he told Charles
Brown, "it is arterial blood;—I cannot be deceived in that colour;—
that drop of blood is my death-warrant."[3] Soon after this event he
apparently offered to release his fiancée, Fanny Brawne, from their
engagement; in the following undated letter, he thanks her for
refusing his offer:

> My sweet love, I shall wait patiently till tomorrow before I see you,
> and in the mean time, if there is any need of such a thing, assure you
> by your Beauty, that whenever I have at any time written on a
> certain unpleasant subject, it has been with your welfare impress'd
> upon my mind. How hurt I should have been had you ever acceded
> to what is, notwithstanding, very reasonable! How much the more
> do I love you from the general result! In my present state of Health I
> feel too much separated from you and could almost speak to you in
> the words of Lorenzo's Ghost to Isabella
>
> > Your Beauty grows upon me and I feel
> > A greater love through all my essence steal.
>
> My greatest torment since I have known you has been the fear of you
> being a little inclined to the Cressid; but that suspicion I dismiss
> utterly and remain happy in the surety of your Love, which I assure
> you is as much a wonder to me as a delight. Send me the words
> "Good night" to put under my pillow. (*Letters,* II, 255–256)

It seems an odd moment for Keats both to confess and to disavow the
jealousy that we know obsessed him from the start of his relationship
with Fanny Brawne; the announcement that he now dismisses utterly
the suspicion that she has been playing Cressida to his Troilus suggests
that his offer to release her was in part a test of her fidelity. But what
mainly interests me in the letter is not the allusion to Shakespearean
(or is it Chaucerian?) jealousy. Before Keats imagines himself as Troilus
and Fanny as Cressida, he imagines Fanny as Isabella and himself as a
ghost, the ghost of the murdered Lorenzo in his own poem *Isabella; or,
The Pot of Basil.*

Isabella is Keats's paraphrase of a tale from Boccaccio's *Decameron.*[4] The
story is simple: a young woman, sister to two merchants (three in Boccaccio's version) falls in love with her brothers' servant Lorenzo; the
brothers discover the affair and, without revealing their discovery, invite
Lorenzo to join them for a ride in the country. When they reach a nearby

forest, the brothers kill Lorenzo and bury him. Isabella, unaware of the crime, laments Lorenzo's absence until his ghost visits her in a dream and describes the grave site. Isabella goes to the forest with her nurse; they dig up the corpse and sever its head, which Isabella carries home and buries in a pot of basil. Eventually her brothers grow suspicious of the attention she lavishes on the plant; they steal the pot, discover the moldered head (now "vile and green with livid spot" [475]), and flee the city (Florence in Keats's version, Messina in Boccaccio's). Isabella dies, deliriously mourning the loss of her beloved pot of basil.

What does it mean for Keats, anticipating his own death, his poetic career over, his marriage plans hopeless, to address his fiancée in the voice of a lover murdered in one of his own poems? From one point of view, no doubt, the letter is merely the decorous elaboration of an invalid's aggressive demand for sympathy. If Keats is Lorenzo then Fanny, like Isabella, is obliged to become obsessed with his loss, to search out his grave, to give up her own life in devotion to some fetishized fragment of his remains. In this respect, the letter suggests the aggressive pathos of a well-known verse fragment that Keats may or may not have intended for an unfinished play:

> This living hand, now warm and capable
> Of earnest grasping, would, if it were cold
> And in the icy silence of the tomb,
> So haunt thy days and chill thy dreaming nights
> That thou would wish thine own heart dry of blood,
> So in my veins red life might stream again,
> And thou be conscience-calm'd. See, here it is—
> I hold it towards you.[5]

Using *Isabella* in the service of such a gesture, Keats might seem to be confirming his own reported judgment that the poem was too "mawkish" for publication (*Letters,* II, 162); he found it "too smokeable" (*Letters,* II, 174)—that is, too easily subject to ridicule. Despite the admiration of Keats's contemporaries—Charles Lamb, for instance, thought *Isabella* "the finest thing" in a volume that also contained *Hyperion* and most of the major odes—modern critics have tended to accept Claude Lee Finney's judgment that *Isabella* represents an inexplicable "reversion" to the sentimentality Keats was supposed to have outgrown after his early association with Leigh Hunt.[6]

But there is another side, both to Keats's letter and to the poem it alludes to. For it is unclear whether Keats is primarily soliciting attention to himself as an object of sympathy or attention to the imagined conjunction of his poem and his life as a composite object of aesthetic "speculation"—Keats's term, I will argue, for what I have been calling "literary interest." The ambiguity lies in part in an uncertainty as to the precise role in which the letter places Fanny: for how can she "be" Isabella and at the same time appreciate the allusion that only *likens* her to Isabella? The letter thus seems, as we say, "overdetermined," the product simultaneously of a personal and a speculative motivation. And that very overdetermination is, once again, the object on which the letter invites its reader to speculate.

A similar logic, in fact, was already at work in the poem. The morning after she is visited by Lorenzo's ghost, Isabella takes a knife and sets out with her nurse to "try" the "inmost of the dream" (342). Presumably, trying the inmost of the dream means testing it to see how far it corresponds to reality, but the expression also foreshadows the literal act of penetration that they will soon perform. They arrive at the grave, and Isabella kneels down beside it, but before plunging her knife into the soil, she hesitates, and this moment of suspense occasions a remarkable digressive stanza on our allegedly universal tendency to linger in cemeteries:

> Who hath not loiter'd in a green church-yard,
>   And let his spirit, like a demon-mole,
> Work through the clayey soil and gravel hard,
>   To see scull, coffin'd bones, and funeral stole;
> Pitying each form that hungry Death hath marr'd,
>   And filling it once more with human soul?
> Ah! this is holiday to what was felt
> When Isabella by Lorenzo knelt.
>   (353–360)

The imagination is figured as a demon-mole; its vaguely ghoulish tendency to burrow its way into other people's graves, where it "pities" and pretends to resuscitate their corpses, is offered as a polite and leisurely alternative to the frantic digging that is about to begin. The contrast between merely speculative and actual digging—between remaining poised above the grave and actually plunging one's knife into the soil—seems almost a deliberate allegory of the distinction Keats drew a year earlier between Shakespearean "negative capability" and the "irritable reaching after fact & reason" Keats associated with writers like Coleridge. A later letter, written to his publisher's adviser, Richard Woodhouse, on 27 October 1818, comes close even to the stanza's language. Keats seems to have threatened to give up writing poetry; he now apologizes, explaining that nothing a poet says should be taken too seriously. For the "poetical Character itself," he writes,

> is not itself—it has no self—it is every thing and nothing—It has no character—it enjoys light and shade; it lives in gusto, be it foul or fair, high or low, rich or poor, mean or elevated—It has as much delight in conceiving an Iago as an Imogen. What shocks the virtuous philosop[h]er, delights the camelion Poet. It does no harm from its relish of the dark side of things any more than from its taste for the bright one; because they both end in speculation. A Poet is the most unpoetical of any thing in existence; because he has no Identity—he is continually in for—and filling some other Body. (*Letters,* I, 118)

The stanza from *Isabella* shows what it means to remain suspended in what Keats calls "speculation"—and what it might mean, at least on the "dark side" of poetic gusto, to "fill some other Body." What is striking about both the letter and the stanza is the way a notion of self-abandonment is connected to a notion of penetrating and "filling" other bodies—as if the self were not so much surrendered as unleashed. One begins to wonder whether negatively capable speculation and an "irritable reaching after fact & reason" are so easily distinguished after all. In the poem, however, the difference between speculative and other kinds of digging is temporarily recaptured in the stanza that immediately follows the poet's digression on cemeteries:

> She gaz'd into the fresh-thrown mould, as though
>   One glance did fully all its secrets tell;
> Clearly she saw, as other eyes would know
>   Pale limbs at bottom of a crystal well;
> Upon the murderous spot she seem'd to grow,
>   Like to a native lily of the dell:
> Then with her knife, all sudden she began
> To dig more fervently than misers can.
>   (361–368)

Unlike the "demon-mole" of speculative imagination, which works its way, as it were, laterally from body to body, lingering to pity and re-animate each marred form, Isabella's vision is a clear and directed

gaze that plunges straight down to its object. The literal act of digging does not so much cancel her imaginary seeing as complete it.
There is a certain turn from hesitation to active appropriation that is
figured in Isabella's double metamorphosis, first into a lily growing
upon "the murderous spot," then into a miser, fervently digging for
her buried treasure. But Isabella's resemblance to a lily was after all
deceptive; if her body was reduced, temporarily, to an image of pas-
toral stasis, her gaze was all the while driving actively into the soil
beneath her. Thus her penetrating gaze and her digging are both
fittingly characterized by the miser's appropriative fervor.

For Isabella is indeed a miser, and not just at the moment that
occasions this explicit simile. The head she proceeds to sever, when
she and the nurse at last arrive at "the kernel of the grave" (383), is
called "the prize" and later "the jewel" (402, 431); like a miser, she
takes it home "in anxious secrecy" (401) and buries it in a garden-
pot. The treasure absorbs all her energy and attention; she seldom
leaves it, even to eat, and of course she dies when it is inevitably
stolen.

In oscillating between the roles of miser and "speculator" (the
modern financial sense of speculation, incidentally, was current
since the latter half of the eighteenth century), Isabella becomes a
rather chillingly precise emblem of the Keatsian "poetical character."[7] Keats had complained about West's painting that, unlike
King Lear, it gave "unpleasantness without any momentous depth of
speculation excited, in which to bury its repulsiveness." To bury
repulsiveness in a depth of speculation—this very odd formula cap-
tures a good deal of the imaginative logic of Keats's Isabella, which
generates erotic and aesthetic profit from the literal burial of a
repulsive object. Conversely, the poem illuminates Keats's rather
idiosyncratic use of the word "speculation." As John Middleton
Murry long ago suggested, Keats may have derived the term from
still another ghost story; Murry cites Macbeth's expression of
wonder at the apparition of his victim Banquo: "Thou hast no speculation in those eyes / Which thou dost glare with."[8] But I think
Murry is mistaken in his insistence that speculation for Keats
means nothing more than "an act of simple vision."[9] Instead I think
the case of Isabella makes it possible to see the degree to which
Keatsian speculation is at once a poetic, an erotic, and an "economic" enterprise. In all three aspects speculation involves a sus-

pension of gratification in the service of an uncertain but possibly greater profit. In this respect—but clearly not in any *ethically* important respect—it contrasts with direct appropriation, figured as greedy theft and miserly hoarding, or as an irritable reaching after fact and reason. But the poem does not merely display the difference between these two ways of acquiring knowledge as well as pleasure and property; it also makes the oscillation between them itself an object of poetic speculation.

As the narrative approaches its conclusion, Isabella's miserliness once again gives way to a strangely abstract version of speculation. Before Lorenzo's ghost arrived to inform her of the murder, Isabella had taken a secret, miserly pleasure in the erotic intensity she derived from Lorenzo's absence: "O misery! / She brooded o'er the luxury alone" (235–236). But this luxurious "misery" turns into something rather different once Isabella acquires possession of Lorenzo's head and literally plants it in her pot of basil:

> And she forgot the stars, the moon, and sun,
>   And she forgot the blue above the trees,
> And she forgot the dells where waters run,
>   And she forgot the chilly autumn breeze;
> She had no knowledge when the day was done,
>   And the new morn she saw not: but in peace
> Hung over her sweet basil evermore,
> And moisten'd it with tears unto the core.
>   (417–424)

The "core" of the basil is of course Lorenzo's head; by refraining from digging it up again, and by hanging over it in this, once again, curiously empty mode of speculation, Isabella gives life to the plant whose beauty and fragrance conceal the head's repulsiveness. Yet the plant is also fertilized, presumably, by the repulsive head itself. But the speculation is not *motivated* by a desire to conceal or forget about its object. What sustains it, apparently, is a peculiar condition of "peace" deriving from the fact that the speculation cancels any thought of a circumstance or action outside itself: what else could one do, after all, with a head in a pot of basil? The stanza is thus a strangely apt depiction of Keatsian speculation as a mode of interest that derives from but replaces a "reaching after" objects, whether those are objects of inquiry or of other forms of desire.

Speculation and Metaphor

A distinction between speculative and more directly purposeful kinds of interest is, of course, a commonplace of post-Kantian aesthetics. But approaching the distinction by way of its Keatsian version has allowed us to see what is wrong with understanding it as involving any morally important difference between an egoistic and an altruistic mode of interest. In the financial and erotic cases, of course, this is obvious: a speculator gives up an immediate payoff but only for the sake of an anticipated, though uncertain, return later on. In the aesthetic case, what one gets in return for a surrender of immediate agency is not a later benefit but a certain mode of experience or consciousness. But if this experience distracts one's attention from the injustice of acquisition, it does nothing to resist or redress that injustice—or its "irritable" cognitive equivalent, the reaching after fact and reason.

In Kantian terms, reaching after fact and reason in Keats's sense is the business of the understanding; it involves an interest in concepts, and the aesthetic is explicitly defined in opposition to conceptual knowledge. This is not the place to go into all the ramifications of this fundamental opposition in Kant's account of the beautiful, but there is one section of the Third Critique—Section 49, "Of the Faculties of the Mind that Constitute Genius"—in which Kant's account seems to bear directly on what Keats calls "speculation." In a way that almost anticipates Keats's complaint about West, the section begins with an observation that certain works of art lack "spirit" *(Geist)*. But what "animating principle of the mind," he asks, is designated by this expression?

> Now I maintain that this principle is no other than the faculty of presenting *aesthetical ideas*. And by an aesthetical idea I understand that representation of the imagination which occasions much thought, without however any definite thought, i.e. any *concept* [*Begriff*], being capable of being adequate to it; it consequently cannot be completely compassed and made intelligible by language.[10]

Kant calls such representations "ideas" because, as he reminds us in the same passage, ideas in his technical usage are representations to which no concepts are "fully adequate . . . as internal intuitions." Thus he calls the idea of an "invisible being," or of "the kingdom of the blessed, hell, eternity, creation, etc.," a "rational idea" because, though

produced by reason, it cannot be captured by the kind of sensible intuition *(Anschauung)* necessary, in Kant's epistemology, for conceptual
knowledge.[11] In any case, a poet tries to "realize" such ideas "to sense";

> or even if he deals with things of which there are examples in
> experience—e.g. death, envy and all vices, also love, fame, and the
> like—he tries, by means of imagination, which emulates the play of
> reason in its quest after a maximum, to go beyond the limits of
> experience and to present them to sense with a completeness of
> which there is no example in nature. *(CJ,* pp. 157–158)

The precise sense in which aesthetic ideas go beyond concepts
becomes clearer (and even more clearly relevant to Keatsian speculation) when Kant introduces his notion of aesthetic *attributes,* which
represent a rational idea by way of "the consequences bound up with it
and its relationship to other concepts." As his discussion of such
attributes gradually makes clear, the main principle involved here is
metaphor:

> Thus Jupiter's eagle with the lightning in its claws is an attribute of
> the mighty king of heaven, as the peacock is of his magnificent
> queen. They do not, like *logical attributes,* represent what lies in our
> concepts of the sublimity and majesty of creation, but something
> different, which gives occasion to the imagination to spread itself
> over a number of kindred representations that arouse more thought
> than can be expressed in a concept determined by words. They
> furnish an *aesthetical idea,* which for that rational idea takes the place
> of logical presentation; and thus, as their proper office, they enliven
> the mind by opening out to it the prospect of an illimitable field of
> kindred representations. *(CJ,* p. 158)

Like painting or sculpture, from which Kant derives these icono-
graphic examples, "poetry and rhetoric also get the spirit that animates
their work simply from the aesthetical attributes of the object, which
accompany the logical and stimulate the imagination, so that it thinks
more by their aid, although in an undeveloped way, than could be
comprehended in a definite form of words" *(CJ,* p. 159).

Kant refrains from specifying the consequences of our concept of
creation that permit its being represented iconographically by Jupiter's
eagle or Juno's peacock. But he gives a poetic example—an excerpt
from a French poem by Frederick the Great—that makes clear the
kind of structure he has in mind. The passage contains a simile that

likens the death of a benevolent man to a sunset: to leave the world "comblé de nos bienfaits" is to be like the setting sun as it diffuses its sweet light. In this way, according to Kant, Frederick

> quickens his rational idea of a cosmopolitan disposition at the end of life by an attribute which the imagination (in remembering all the pleasures of a beautiful summer day that are recalled at its close by a serene evening) associates with that representation, and which excites a number of sensations and secondary representations for which no expression is found. (*CJ*, p. 159)

Notice that, on Kant's reading, the simile comparing the disposition to a sunset involves a metaphorical projection of the disposition as possessing the sunset as its "attribute." The connection between a "rational idea" and its "aesthetic attribute" thus appears to lie (though Kant doesn't say so explicitly) in a particular kind of metaphor. As John Hodgson has pointed out in analyzing an account of similar figures by Coleridge, the metaphor is based on a prior metonymical substitution, for each of the two terms, of effect for cause.[12] Thus the metaphorical projection of divine power as Jupiter's eagle is based on a prior metonymy signifying divine power by effects (for instance, awe) resembling the effects associated with an eagle grasping lightning. And the simile describing a cosmopolitan disposition as a beautiful sunset is based on a metonymical substitution, for each term, of the serenity it produces in someone who contemplates it.

What sets the mind in motion and keeps it moving is the irreducibility, in the case of rational ideas, of metonymy. There is no way to read back from our concepts of the various effects associated with the subject of a rational idea to a *concept* of what the rational idea represents. The effects, in a sense, are all we have. The poet links those effects to the effects of something we *can* conceptualize. The resulting metaphor gives the rational idea a definite representational form it would otherwise lack; borrowing a phrase from Janet Martin Soskice, we might say that it gives reflection on the idea a definite "semantic placement."[13] But such reflection can never yield a definite cognition, since the content of the representation (despite the definiteness of its form) remains an "illimitable field" of associated effects, that is, "sensations and secondary representations" for which no definite verbal expression can be found.

The contrast here between a definite semantic placement and the lack of any definite cognitive content points to a surprising parallel between the Kantian account of poetic genius and a controversial recent account of metaphorical meaning. According to Donald Davidson's already classic essay "What Metaphors Mean," a metaphor *has* no meaning—and therefore no "definite cognitive content"—beyond the literal meaning of the sentence in which the metaphor occurs.[14] "What distinguishes metaphor," according to Davidson,

> is not meaning but use—in this it is like assertion, hinting, lying, promising, or criticizing. And the special use to which we put language in metaphor is not—cannot be—to "say something" special, no matter how indirectly. For a metaphor *says* only what shows on its face—usually a patent falsehood or an absurd truth. And this plain truth needs no paraphrase—its meaning is given in the literal meaning of the words. ("WMM," p. 259)

Davidson allows for a certain notion of "metaphorical truth," but the truth of which a metaphor is capable is no part of the semantic content of the metaphor itself: "Metaphor does lead us to notice what might not otherwise be noticed, and there is no reason, I suppose, not to say these visions, thoughts, and feelings inspired by the metaphor are true or false" ("WMM," p. 257).

But why not treat the truths revealed by the metaphor as part of its semantic content? Why not call the visions, thoughts, and feelings a metaphor inspires its metaphorical meaning? Davidson's answer is crucially relevant to the connection between metaphor and the kind of negatively capable agency involved in literary speculation. If his account is right, Davidson argues,

> what we attempt in "paraphrasing" a metaphor cannot be to give its meaning, for that lies on the surface; rather we attempt to evoke what the metaphor brings to our attention. I can imagine someone granting this and shrugging it off as no more than an insistence on restraint in using the word "meaning." This would be wrong. The central error about metaphor is most easily attacked when it takes the form of a theory of metaphorical meaning, but behind that theory, and statable independently, is the thesis that associated with a metaphor is a definite cognitive content that its author wishes to convey and that the interpreter must grasp if he is to get the message. This theory is false . . . whether or not we call the purported cognitive content a meaning. ("WMM," p. 262)

There is, it seems to me, an undeniable difficulty in Davidson's account, and the quickest way to get at the difficulty is to point out that, at least in the case of ordinary metaphors, not everything a metaphor might make someone notice counts as relevant to an understanding of the metaphor in question. Davidson may be right in saying that we are "nudged" by metaphor "into noting" resemblances ("WMM," p. 253), but if so, then, as Soskice points out, "we are nudged in a certain direction": "Unless he can explain why the failure of a literal reading should issue in a recognition of a *particular* similarity, his theory cannot supplant one in which the implications are regarded as being, in some sense, part of the meaning of the metaphor."[15] And what makes the question of relevance practically urgent is that fact that, as Max Black remarks in a reply to Davidson's essay, we "take the metaphor's author to be committed to its implications."[16]

Yet it seems implausible to suggest that a metaphor's author has in mind some particular implication or set of implications; for if so, Davidson asks, why should it be "so hard to decide, even in the case of the simplest metaphors, what the content of the metaphor should be"? ("WMM," p. 262). And in any case, if the author had some definite content in mind, why did he/she bother to resort to metaphor? One way to respond to these questions might be to challenge the notion that what an author has to have in mind, in order to have a meaning in mind, is something more or less definite.

Such a challenge appears in the intriguing account of meaning advanced by Dan Sperber and Deirdre Wilson in their book *Relevance.*[17] Sperber and Wilson criticize what they take to be a fundamental mistake in the field of "pragmatics" (that is, "the study of the interpretation of utterances"; *Relevance,* p. 10). The mistake is to suppose that pragmatics "should be concerned purely with the recovery of an enumerable set of assumptions, some explicitly expressed, others implicitly conveyed, but all individually intended by the speaker." Against this view, Sperber and Wilson argue that

> there is a continuum of cases, from implicatures which the hearer was specifically intended to recover to implicatures which were merely intended to be made manifest, and to further modifications of the mutual cognitive environment of speaker and hearer that the speaker only intended in the sense that she intended her utterance to be relevant, and hence to have rich and not entirely foreseeable cognitive effects. (*Relevance,* p. 201)

This account expands the notion of meaning beyond the sort of definite content that Davidson has in mind. But it might seem to do so only by contradicting the claim, defended in the previous chapter, that the only plausible object of interpretation is a content intended by the writer or speaker. Does it? Are Sperber and Wilson suggesting that the utterance's meaning goes beyond the speaker's intention to embrace effects supplied by the hearer alone? The trouble with such a suggestion would parallel the problem we detected in a proposal simply to replace the intended content of *Paradise Lost* with a better content: once one decides to count unintended implicatures as part of the utterance's meaning, then the meaning of every utterance becomes trivially infinite. For sooner or later, the thoughts triggered by any utterance can lead *anywhere*.

Here, however, are two ways of interpreting Sperber and Wilson's account that would preserve the connection between the utterance's meaning and the speaker's intention: (1) we might decide that implicatures count as parts of the utterance's meaning as long as they are "covered" by the speaker's intention, that is, as long as they belong to some *set* of implicatures intended by the speaker; or (2) we might treat all implicatures that are not specifically intended by the speaker merely as accidental *effects* of the utterance, whether or not such accidental effects turn out to be relevant. The trouble with (2) is that it defines intended meaning so narrowly as to render it irrelevant to a vast range of the actions speakers actually take themselves to be performing. Adopting (1), on the other hand, requires expanding the notion of what counts as an intended meaning to include thoughts that are not identical but (in the right way) related to the thoughts a speaker specifically had in mind. And in fact I see no reason not to expand the notion of an intended meaning in exactly this way; it seems clear that speakers do, in fact, frequently accept as correct interpretations of their utterances various implicatures that they did not specifically have in mind when they framed the utterances in question—provided, once again, that such implicatures belong to the *set* of implicatures they *did* have in mind. As Sperber and Wilson suggest, "the communicator must have in mind a representation of the set of assumptions . . . which she intends to make manifest or more manifest to the audience. However, to have a representation of a set of assumptions it is not necessary to have a representation of each assumption in the set" (p. 58). Thus a speaker can have in mind a

"cognitive content" in Davidson's sense without having in mind everything that belongs to the cognitive content in question.

So far, then, there is nothing in Sperber and Wilson's account specifically of metaphor that contradicts a claim that an utterance only
means what its speaker intends it to mean, or that prevents a metaphor
from having such an intended meaning just because it is hard to
specify exactly that meaning's content. And in fact, to interpret a metaphor, on their account, is still to figure out what a speaker is getting
at. Nevertheless, metaphor *does* involve a certain transfer of agency
from speaker to hearer, and to see why is to see the sense in which their
account converges, at least in some degree, with Kant's and
Davidson's.

In Sperber and Wilson's view, an utterance's being literal is not a
matter of its having a special content but only of its having the same
"propositional form" as the thought it represents, where a representation's "propositional form" is the form in virtue of which it represents
a definite state of affairs that would make that representation either
true or false (*Relevance,* pp. 72–73, 233). And metaphor is just one of
many cases in which an utterance's propositional form differs from that
of the thought the speaker aims to communicate. But what is the
point of producing an utterance whose propositional form does *not*
match the propositional form of the thought one intends to convey?
According to Sperber and Wilson, "the element of indirectness" in a
non-literal utterance must be "offset by some increase in contextual
effects." If something prevents the hearer from taking the utterance
literally, then her attempt to give it a "relevant" meaning will cause
her to look for a "range of further contextual implications" that she
would not have to look for if the utterance could be taken literally.
Even in the case of a stereotypical metaphor like "This room is a
pigsty," the fact that the speaker resorted to the indirectness of metaphor—the fact that she did not just say "This room is filthy"—
instructs a hearer to go beyond the simple association of pigs and filth;
the hearer will conclude that the speaker meant "something more . . .
an image, say, of filthiness and tidiness beyond the norm, beyond what
could have been satisfactorily conveyed by saying merely 'This room is
very filthy and untidy' " (*Relevance,* pp. 235–236).

As this unpromising example already makes clear (and this is, for
my purposes, the most important feature of Sperber and Wilson's
account), indirectness shifts the burden of communicative agency in

some degree from the speaker to the hearer: "The wider the range of possible conclusions, the weaker the implicatures, and the more the hearer must share the responsibility for deriving them." Furthermore, according to Sperber and Wilson,

> The wider the range of potential implicatures and the greater the hearer's responsibility for constructing them, the more poetic the effect, the more creative the metaphor. A good creative metaphor is precisely one in which a variety of contextual effects can be retained and understood as weakly implicated by the speaker. In the richest and most successful cases, the hearer or reader can go beyond just exploring the immediate context . . . , accessing a wide area of knowledge, adding metaphors of his own as interpretations of possible developments he is not ready to go into, and getting more and more very weak implicatures, with suggestions for still further processing. The result is a quite complex picture, for which the hearer [or reader] has to take a large part of the responsibility, but the discovery of which has been triggered by the writer. (*Relevance,* pp. 236–237)

In an important sense, what Sperber and Wilson have provided here is an updated version of Keatsian "negative capability." By suspending a direct imposition of communicative purpose—and therefore tolerating a significant degree of uncertainty in the communicative situation—the writer "triggers" in the reader an activity of imaginative exploration that it seems reasonable enough to call "speculation." But the shift, in Sperber and Wilson's own metaphors, from the sharing of responsibility to the triggering of discovery introduces a certain ambiguity into their account of what makes a metaphor "poetic."[18] Do the poet and reader share a responsibility for the communication between them of the poet's thoughts? Is this account, in other words, still consistent with the intentionalist reading of Sperber and Wilson's theory that I offered above? Or does the process of discovery at some point leave the poet's intention behind?

I see no reason to try to give the last question a general answer. For I see no reason why the activity triggered by a poetic metaphor—or indeed by any literary representation—should take the form of an attempt to *interpret* the representation. Even if, as his critics argue, Davidson is wrong in excluding the indirect communication of a writer's thoughts from the category of what he is willing to call meaning, he is right in seeing that there is an interest in metaphor that goes beyond any interest in figuring out what thoughts the writer intends to communicate. But the possibility of this interest does not depend on the metaphor's lack of "cognitive content." As soon as one gives up the notion that intending to communicate necessarily means intending to communicate a determinate set of representations, there is no reason to deny that *interpreting* a metaphor involves discovering the cognitive content the writer intends to communicate. For in Sperber and Wilson's terms, cognitive content can embrace "implicatures" that belong to the "set of assumptions" the writer has in mind, even if the writer does not have in mind each particular member of the set.

Notice that, in this respect, the content of a metaphor is similar to the content of an imagined "world" as described in Chapter 1. Just as an author need not intend every state of affairs belonging to an imagined world in order to count as intending to present that world, so it isn't necessary for a metaphor's author to intend each assumption that belongs to the set of assumptions the metaphor is intended to communicate. In both cases, the reader is free to extrapolate on the basis of what the author has explicitly indicated. But such extrapolation, in both cases, will only continue to count as interpretation as long as the interpreter has reason to think that what she arrives at continues to belong to the content intended by the author.

But why should interest stop at interpretation? Once a reader has been "nudged" to notice analogies, why stop at noticing analogies that can be plausibly assigned to the set of assumptions the author intended? Why not go on to notice, for instance, analogies between a metaphor's intended content and whatever else there is to notice—just as I went on, at the end of the first chapter, to notice the (surely unintended) analogy between the (alleged) failure of Milton's own agency and the failure of a certain picture of agency within Milton's poem?

In Kant's account, the turn from interpretation to speculation was based on the irreducible indefiniteness of one of the metaphor's terms. The advantage of Sperber and Wilson's account is that it shows why *any* source of indefiniteness can trigger a speculative interest that supplants an interest in figuring out what an author, and therefore the author's representation, means. What remains to be explained is why a speculative interest that goes beyond an interest in a representation's meaning should nevertheless remain bound—indeed, like Isabella, more bound than ever—to the representation that excites it.

3

The Concrete Universal

Absorbing Interest

The previous two chapters have concerned attempts to locate the uniqueness of literary meaning in the (allegedly) peculiar status of authorial agency, which is conceived as failing, or else as suspending itself, in ways that enable the meaning it produces to exceed authorial intention. In both cases, however, an apparent shift of attention from the author to someone or something else showed a paradoxical tendency to reverse itself; for the very act of thematizing authorial failure or self-abnegation elicited a heightened interest in the author's agency. The frequency of such a thematic reversal may even give the impression that displacements of authorial agency are really aimed at generating a kind of interest that will end up, sooner or later, in the authorial account.

In the long run, however, the phenomenon of thematic reversal is a more general source of worry about (as well as celebration of) the literary than is the particular problem of authorial agency. The problem in its more general form arises as soon as one asks, as the Western critical tradition has asked since Plato, the following question: What does it mean to be interested in a literary representation? Asked in that way, the question is obviously too abstract, but it can be sharpened if one asks what it means to be *more* interested in a representation than in what it represents—more interested in a story than in what the story is about, in a poem than in what it imitates, in a symbol than in what the symbol ostensibly refers to. Sharpening the question in this way brings out a certain suspicion that was perhaps already implicit in it: a suspicion that the interest provoked by an aesthetic representation comes at the expense of an interest in the very objects to which the representation might seem to direct one's attention. "The painting looks like a landscape," W. K. Wimsatt writes, "but we rest in the looks and need not be moved to go outdoors. The tragedy is about murder, but we rest short of wishing to save the victim or punish the criminal."[1]

The notion that art and nature compete for our attention is not, at first sight, very surprising. If one's interest in a representation merely *competes* with one's interest in what is represented, the specificity of literary interest, as the tradition I am considering understands it, can be easily and rather trivially accounted for; it consists in a simple oscillation between competing objects of attention. Sometimes our attention is drawn to an actual murder, sometimes to a tragedy in which an imaginary murder is played out. But the oscillation is complicated by the fact that one kind of interest—interest in the representation itself—is not just an alternative to but is at the same time *dependent* on the other. It is, in other words, not just a competitor but a parasite. This point is foregrounded in a lucid formula that Wimsatt adds to the remarks quoted above: "In short, the aesthetic symbol *absorbs the interest of its referents into itself* and contains it in an impractical stasis" (*VI,* p. 273; emphasis added). Surprisingly, given his role as perhaps the foremost theoretician of American New Criticism, Wimsatt does not here imagine that the aesthetic symbol has any particular interest of its own; whatever interest it does have it seems to acquire, once again parasitically, by ingesting the interest originally possessed by its ostensible object. Dropping the biological metaphor, one might say that, in the case of the aesthetic symbol, the ordinary teleology of referential interest is reversed, as the referent becomes the means by which the symbol provokes an interest in itself.

To say that an aesthetic symbol "provokes an interest in itself" is to say nothing about how it does so, or why the fact that it does so should have played so prominent a role in traditional debates about the epistemological and ethical value of the literary. In what follows, I propose to move toward the former question initially by way of the latter. In later sections, I will develop an account of literary structure that may explain, if it does not quite answer, the traditional suspicion that there

is something disturbingly impractical, or even anti-practical, about
our interest in literary artifacts.

The Socratic Scandal

The reversal of direction suggested by Wimsatt's formula is, as I have
already suggested, a persistent—indeed, in some respects a founda-
tional—theme in Western criticism. It frequently takes the slightly
different form we have encountered in the previous chapters; the form,
once again, of a shift of attention not from the object to the representation itself but from the object to the *agent* of representation (from the
matter of poetry to the poet). This version of the teleological reversal is
especially obvious in a critical tradition to which Wimsatt himself was
notoriously hostile: the Longinian. Longinus was in fact singled out,
though only for disapproval, by Wimsatt and Monroe C. Beardsley in a
pivotal moment of their essay "The Intentional Fallacy":

> It is not so much a historical statement as a definition to say that the
> intentional fallacy is a romantic one. When a rhetorician of the first
> century A.D. writes: "Sublimity is the echo of a great soul," or when
> he tells us that "Homer enters into the sublime actions of his heroes"
> and "shares the full inspiration of the combat," we shall not be
> surprised to find this rhetorician considered as a distant harbinger of
> romanticism and greeted in the warmest terms by Saintsbury. One
> may wish to argue whether Longinus should be called romantic, but
> there can hardly be a doubt that in one important way he is. (*VI*,
> p. 6)

Given this apparent opposition, it is worth noticing how closely the
Longinian passages cited here by Wimsatt and Beardsley resemble
Wimsatt's own account of literary interest. Homer, in writing about
Ajax, is really displaying the greatness of his own soul, which is in one
sense the proper object of Longinian admiration. On the other hand,
an interest in Homer's greatness cannot simply dispense with an
interest in the objects Homer is representing, since Homer's greatness
is only visible in—and is indeed inseparable from—the poet's capacity
to enter into the sublime actions of his heroes. The only way to charac-
terize Homer's own sublimity is to describe it in the very same terms
that Homer applies to his objects: "In truth," Longinus writes (in a
sentence partly quoted by Wimsatt and Beardsley), "Homer in these
cases shares the full inspiration of the combat, and it is neither more

nor less than true of the poet himself that 'Mad rageth he as Ares the shaker of spears, or as mad flames leap / Wild-wasting from hill unto hill,' " and so on.[2] There are, however, several ways of understanding what Longinus is saying here. This might be nothing more than an elaborate rhetorical compliment, hyperbolically positing an analogy between Homer's imaginative power and the superhuman passions of his heroes. Or it might be understood as an explanatory claim, in keeping with Longinus's explicit aim in this chapter of exploring the chief of the five principal sources or conditions of the sublime, "namely elevation of mind." "For it is not possible that [people] with mean and servile ideas and aims prevailing throughout their lives should produce anything that is admirable and worthy of immortality."[3] But a third possibility—that the poet's own elevation of mind is the actual object of sublime representation—emerges unmistakably in the Longinian revival in the seventeenth and eighteenth centuries. Here, for instance, are the well-known lines in which Pope uses Longinus's mode of praising Homer to praise Longinus himself:

> Thee, bold *Longinus!* all the Nine inspire,
> And bless *their Critick* with a *Poet's Fire.*
> An ardent *Judge,* who Zealous in his Trust,
> With *Warmth* gives Sentence, yet is always *Just;*
> Whose *own Example* strengthens all his Laws,
> And *Is himself* that great *Sublime* he draws.[4]

The equation can of course be accounted for in strictly rhetorical terms—the sublime in this case may not be literally identical to the critic's genius—but a rhetorical reduction is less plausible in the case of Edward Young's version of the same equation in his *Conjectures on Original Composition* (1759). Discussing our ignorance "of the dimensions of the human mind," "even of our own," Young points to

> the sudden eruption of some men out of perfect obscurity into public admiration, on the strong impulse of some animating occasion; not more to the world's great surprise, than their own. Few authors of distinction but have experienced something of this nature, at the first beamings of their yet unsuspected genius on their hitherto dark composition. The writer starts at it, as at a lucid meteor in the night, is much surprised, can scarce believe it true. During his happy confusion, it may be said to him, as to Eve at the lake,

> "What there thou seest, fair creature, is thyself."[5]

Eve looking into the lake in the moments following her creation: does she fall in love with the image of herself, or should we read God's equation to mean that what she falls in love with is what she herself really is, namely, an image? Given the doctrinal assumptions under-lying Milton's epic, the equation of image and person makes all too perfect sense: Eve is supposed to learn that she is, after all, only an image, and the voice next promises to take her

> where no shadow stays
> Thy coming, and thy soft embraces, he
> Whose image thou art, him thou shalt enjoy
> Inseparably thine, to him shalt bear
> Multitudes like thyself . . . [6]
>   (IV.470–474)

—that is, the voice will lead her to Adam, who is substance to her shadow, and who will enable her to produce innumerable images of herself as compensation for her own reduction to an image.[7] Part of what is striking about Young's use of the passage is that he chooses, as an emblem of authorial self-consciousness, an experience of self-dis-covery by a character whose sex ideologically requires the subordina-tion of her consciousness. Later on, in a discussion of Wimsatt's treatment of the figures of Falstaff and Cleopatra, I will suggest a reason why accounts of the special conditions of literary representation tend to involve the attribution of self-awareness to figures traditionally deprived of full consciousness. At this point, however, what is impor-tant to notice is the way Milton's episode, via Young's allusion to it, adds a further complication to the Longinian account of literary refer-ence. The parasitism revealed by Wimsatt's formula now seems curi-ously mutual, since a poet's genius is displayed in a capacity to identify with what turns out to be already a reflection of the poet's self. Poetic agency absorbs the interest of its object into itself, but the interest of its object is already an interest in poetic agency. And yet, as we have already seen, an interest in poetic agency is inseparable from an interest in the represented object whose greatness the poet can only reflect.

The perception that literary interest is involved in a relation of mutual parasitism—that is, an oscillation between objects whose interest derives from their relation to each other—is by no means an invention of Longinus or of neo-Longinians. A version of the same perception lies at the heart of the Platonic/Socratic attack on poetry.[8] And this point is of more than antiquarian interest, since Socrates' account of this perception elaborates it in ways that move the Longinian paradox even closer to the dominant emphases of the kind of formalism exemplified by Wimsatt. For it is Plato's Socrates, not Longinus, who provides the crucial link between a psychological analysis of literary interest and the claim that literary language is logically or metaphysically unique, above all because of its capacity to generate what Wimsatt will call "the concrete universal." Before returning to Wimsatt, it is consequently worth retracing the steps of Socrates' quasi-satirical analysis of poetic agency in Plato's dialogue *Ion*.

Socrates' initial target in this dialogue is neither poetry nor poets but the pretensions of a certain "rhapsode," the professional reciter of Homer who gives the dialogue its title. Ion has just won first prize in a competition among rhapsodes at the festival of Aesculapius in Epidaurus. Socrates at first pretends to envy Homeric rhapsodes, in part because of the knowledge they must possess of this "best and most divine" of poets. Socrates is certain, he says, that "no man can become a good rhapsode who does not understand the meaning of the poet. For the rhapsode ought to interpret the mind of the poet to his hearers, but how can he interpret him well unless he knows what he means?" Ion answers with typically self-exposing vanity:

> Very true, Socrates; interpretation has certainly been the most laborious part of my art; and I believe myself able to speak about Homer better than any man; and that neither Metrodorus of Lampsacus, nor Stesismbrotus of Thasos, nor Glaucon, nor anyone else who ever was, had as good ideas about Homer as I have, or as many. (*Ion* 530b-d)[9]

By isolating the phrase "or as many" at the end of the speech, Jowett's translation makes obvious what is only fleetingly present at this point in the original dialogue—the Greek text merely has Ion say that no one else has as "many and good ideas" *(pollas kai kalas dianoias)* as he has. But Jowett's revision will prove to be justified by the essential role that the scandal of poetic multiplicity will eventually play in Socrates' critique. For the moment, Socrates ignores Ion's claim to intellectual fecundity or, implicitly, *universality,* and starts a line of questioning that quickly pushes Ion in the opposite direction, that is, into an acknowledgment of the extreme narrowness or *particularity* of his expertise (I am using the terms "universality" and "particularity" here not in any Platonic sense but to indicate the logical connection between Socrates' attack and certain modern claims about the status of literary representation):

> SOCRATES I should like to ask you a question: Does your art extend
>   to Hesiod and Archilochus, or to Homer only?
> ION To Homer only; he is in himself quite enough. (531a)

But Socrates wonders how an interpreter's skill can be limited to a *single* poet. After all, poets sometimes disagree when they treat the same themes. If an interpreter can tell when one poet is singing well about something, why can't the same interpreter tell whether another poet is singing badly about the same subject? For consider the other arts: suppose two speakers are discussing arithmetic or the wholesomeness of food; won't someone who recognizes the better speaker in these cases also recognize the worse? If so (and Ion cheerfully endorses each step in Socrates' reasoning), then Ion, who knows when Homer is speaking well, must surely be equally expert in recognizing when other poets speak less well of the same things. And since "almost all poets do speak of the same things" (532b)—human society, the various classes of people, the generations of gods and heroes, and so on (531c-d)—won't Ion admit that he must be "equally skilled in Homer and in other poets" (532B)? Here Ion balks; "Why then, Socrates," he asks, of course naïvely, "do I lose attention and have absolutely no ideas of the least value and practically fall asleep when anyone speaks of any other poet; but when Homer is mentioned, I wake up at once and am all attention and have plenty to say?" (532b-c).

This is the question toward which Socrates' argument has been driving all along, and his reply for the first time formulates the charge that the rest of the dialogue will for the most part only elaborate: "The reason, my friend, is not hard to guess. No one can fail to see that you speak of Homer without any art or knowledge. If you were able to speak of him by rules of art, you would have been able to speak of all other poets; for poetry is a whole."

At this point Socrates appears to be—indeed, is pretending to be—contrasting the particularity and hence irrationality of the rhapsode's skill with the wholeness of poetry itself, though the target of Socrates' critique will soon expand beyond the rhapsode to include poetic agency in general. For now, it is crucial to notice exactly how the themes of particularity and irrationality (though not, of course, named as such by Socrates) have been connected. In the case of an art, a genuine *technē* like divination, arithmetic, or cookery—and painting, sculpture, and music are quickly added to Socrates' list—the content of the art is universal, that is, it remains the same no matter who practices the art in question. This is why Socrates focuses on cases in which two practitioners of the same art disagree; since the content of the art remains whatever it is, it provides a universal standard against which the relative merits of particular performers can be judged. Precisely because its content is fixed, in other words, the agents who practice a genuine art are mutually comparable and, for the same reason, replaceable. If what counts is the content of the art itself—if that is what governs speech about the art—then it cannot matter very much who does the talking. But if a fixity and thus a universality of content entail an indifference to particular agency, then surely, Socrates reasons, a fixity of *agency* must signal an absence of any fixed or universal content. Since the rhapsode's art, on Ion's own enthusiastic admission, is bound to a single irreplaceable agent, the poet whose particular name is the only one that can arouse his interest, then the inevitable inference, on the logic Socrates has been developing, is that his art is devoid of any rationally accessible content.

The only remaining step is to claim that the art of poetry itself is similarly devoid of content, indeed that it consists of nothing more than a power to bind people to a fixed source of agency. Which is exactly what Socrates proceeds to do, by means of an extraordinary and notorious simile:

> The gift which you possess of speaking excellently about Homer is not an art, but, as I was just saying, an inspiration; there is a divinity moving you [literally a divine power, *theia dunamis*], like that contained in the stone which Euripides calls a magnet, but which is commonly known as the stone of Heraclea. This stone not only attracts iron rings, but also imparts to them a similar power of attracting other rings; and sometimes you may see a number of pieces of iron and rings suspended from one another so as to form quite a long chain; and all of them derive their power of suspension from the original stone. In like manner the Muse first of all inspires [people] herself; and from these inspired persons a chain of other persons is suspended, who take the inspiration. For all good poets,

epic as well as lyric, compose their beautiful poems not by art, but because they are inspired and possessed. (533d-e)

Now that the analogy between rhapsode and poet is explicitly drawn, Socrates proceeds to connect poetic agency with the same irrational particularity that he earlier associated with rhapsodic interpretation:

> Many are the noble words in which poets speak concerning [human actions]; but like yourself when speaking about Homer, they do not speak of them by any rules of art: they are simply inspired to utter that to which the Muse impels them, and that only; and when inspired, one of them will make dithyrambs, another hymns of praise, another choral strains, another epic or iambic verses, but not one of them is of any account in the other kinds. For not by art does the poet sing, but [once again] by power divine; had he learned by rules of art, he would have known how to speak not of one theme only, but of all. (534b-c)

If rhapsodic interpretation is fixed or particularized by its dependence on a particular poet, poetic agency itself seems to be particularized by its dependence on the (relative) particularity of what we would call poetic genre, which is to say—though Socrates lacks the Aristotelian equipment to say this—the particularity of literary form. Actually Socrates, in stopping at genre, stops short of supposing (as a later formalist might) that poetic agency is bound to the form of an individual poem. But it is nevertheless particularized (by genre) in a way that sets it apart from the kind of agency appropriate to the genuine arts.

The connection between particularity of agency and particularity of form, though only glimpsed in Plato's dialogue, will turn out to have a decisive importance in Wimsatt's formalism. For Socrates, however, the dependence on formal particularity is mainly interesting as a symptom of irrationality, an irrationality he identifies, no doubt ironically, with the presence of divine inspiration. But the appeal to inspiration, however seriously or playfully it is intended, soon gives way to a rather different account of the mechanism that particularizes literary agency. After forcing Ion to acknowledge that rhapsodes are merely "interpreters of interpreters" (535a)—they interpret the poets, who in turn interpret the voice of the gods—Socrates switches directions, turning from the origins of the rhapsode's power to the rhapsode's effect on his own audience. Socrates' apparent aim at this point is to identify poetry with madness; for how else can one explain the bizarre phenomenon of the rhapsode and his audience weeping or looking panic-stricken in the midst of a joyous festival? But this question, whether or not intentionally, exposes the mechanism of poetic contagion, the mechanism by which the signs of these mad or at least inappropriate passions are transferred from poet to rhapsode to audience: a mechanism no longer of inspiration but of imitation, or, recalling the discussion of Longinus, of identification.

Ostensibly Socrates is looking for additional evidence that the rhapsode is divinely inspired or, what amounts to the same thing, irrational:

> SOCRATES I wish you would frankly tell me, Ion, what I am going to ask of you: When you produce the greatest effect upon the audience in the recitation of some striking passage, such as the apparition of Odysseus leaping forth on the floor, recognized by the suitors and shaking out his arrows at his feet, or the description of Achilles springing upon Hector, or the sorrows of Andromache, Hecuba, or Priam,—are you in your right mind? Are you not carried out of yourself, and does not your soul in an ecstasy seem to be among the persons or places of which you are speaking, whether they are in Ithaca or in Troy or whatever may be the scene of the poem?
>
> ION That proof strikes home to me, Socrates. For I must frankly confess that at the tale of pity my eyes are filled with tears, and when I speak of horrors, my hair stands on end and my heart throbs. (535b-c)

Apart from its dialogic form, this passage might as well have been written by Longinus, and equally Longinian is the way Socrates now shifts from the rhapsode's identification with his objects to the mimetic contagion by which that identification extends to the rhapsode's audience.[10] According to Longinus, when we hear a sublime discourse "our soul is uplifted . . . ; it takes a proud flight, and is filled with joy and vaunting, as though it had itself produced what it has heard."[11] The same principle emerges when Socrates asks Ion whether he is aware that his identification with Homer's characters provokes an analogous identification on the part of his audience. Socrates is leading up to the conclusion that the spectator is merely the last of the rings suspended from the Homeric magnet. But Ion's answer for once appears to go beyond the part that Socrates has scripted for him:

SOCRATES And are you aware that you produce similar effects on most of the spectators?

ION Only too well; for I look down upon them from the stage, and behold the various emotions of pity, wonder, sternness, stamped upon their countenances when I am speaking: and I am obliged to give my very best attention to them; for if I make them cry I myself shall laugh, and if I make them laugh I myself shall cry, when the time of payment arrives. (535d-e)

Oddly enough, Socrates ignores Ion's confession that he is mainly interested in turning a profit, despite the opportunity it would seem to provide for still another deprecation of the rhapsode's art. But it is perhaps no accident that Socrates lets this opportunity slip. After all, Ion, without really knowing it, has stumbled upon a potential refutation of Socrates' claim that rhapsodic agency is a matter of involuntary inspiration. For it now turns out the rhapsode knows what he is doing; far from being absorbed in his identification with the agents depicted by Homer, he is sufficiently detached from them to notice whether the interest he is provoking is likely to pay off. To at least some extent, then, Ion as professional performer is forced to tailor his imitations of Homer's heroes to the nature and degree of imitation he perceives in his audience; there is thus a certain reflective feedback in what Socrates has wanted to represent as a one-directional and involuntary transfer of energy. Poetic identification, in other words, is not simply a matter of involuntary ignorance but is partly also, thanks to the reflective possibilities introduced by the structure of imitation, a form of lying, of willful pretense or insincerity. Hence the dilemma of rhapsodic (and, by implication, poetic) agency: it is either too absorbed in its object or not absorbed enough. This apparently anomalous moment in the dialogue thus introduces an oscillation between self-forgetting and self-reflexiveness that closely parallels the oscillation between reference and self-reference we have encountered in the Longinian tradition and in Wimsatt's formalism.

To this point the dialogue has been concerned to establish the irrationality of poetry by exposing the particularity and fixity of poetic agency. But this is only one side of the Platonic/Socratic critique. For in another sense the trouble with poetry is not that it is too concrete or particular but that it is too universal—so universal in its claims as to be in fact devoid of content. This second major phase of the argument (536e ff.) is easily summarized; Socrates merely lists the various arts on which Homer seems to comment—charioteering, medicine, fishing, prophecy, navigation, spinning, cowherding, horsemanship, playing the lyre, generalship—and then asks who is likely to be a better judge of what Homer is saying about these arts, a rhapsode or a specialist in the art in question. Ion proves unable to name a single art in which his specialization in the study of Homer provides an expertise not inferior to, and indeed parasitic on, the expertise of others. Although Socrates never directly questions Homer's own expertise in any of the arts mentioned, the implication is clear: the very multiplicity of the subjects covered by poetry counts against the possibility that poetry provides access to any form of knowledge not better sought elsewhere.

This final turn in the argument places us, at last, in a position to spell out the connection Socrates is making between the scandal of poetic agency and the anomalous relation between universality and particularity that distinguishes poetry from the other arts. In the case of a genuine art or *techné,* the subject matter is properly universal, in the sense that it provides a universal standard against which the efforts of particular practitioners can be judged. At the same time, however, the subject matter of a true art is properly particular, in the sense that its identity is fixed by its own particular laws, which is why an experienced practitioner can speak about it with more authority than can a parasitic dilettante like Ion. In the case of poetry, the relation between universality and particularity is similarly complicated, but complicated in a way that, from Socrates' perspective, can only seem pathological. The subject matter of poetry is indeed (in one sense) universal, since poetic representation implicitly claims a mastery of all the other arts. But this is a bad or trivial kind of universality, based on an ignorance of, or indifference to, the particular laws that properly distinguish one true art from another. If poetry is badly universal, it is also badly particular, since the access it provides to its trivially universal content proceeds irrationally, by way of a fixed, particular line of agency. And that fixed line of agency is really nothing more than a sequence of imitations, that is, a sequence of arbitrary acts of identification with an agency not properly one's own.

Meaning and Experience

"Whether or not one believes in universals, one may see the persistence in literary criticism of a theory that poetry presents the concrete and the universal, or the individual and the universal, or an object which in a mysterious and special way is both highly general and highly particular." So Wimsatt writes in his seminal essay "The Concrete Universal" (*VI*, p. 71). Since he is only interested in honorific applications of this notion, he never mentions Plato. He starts his survey of previous accounts of poetry's peculiar status with Aristotle, then goes on to cite Plotinus, Cicero, Du Fresnoy, Edward Young, Joseph Warton, Johnson, Reynolds, Blake, Kant, Hegel, Coleridge, and Ruskin, observing that "in one terminology or another this idea of a concrete universal is found in most metaphysical aesthetic of the eighteenth and nineteenth centuries" (*VI*, p. 72). His twentieth-century examples are Bergson and Croce, as well as Ransom and Tate and, by the implication of their critical practice, Empson, Blackmur, and Brooks. I am not suggesting that, by ignoring Socrates' hostility to what others praise, Wimsatt is simply idealizing the tradition or granting it a false consistency; he is fully aware of sharp disagreements among the critics he cites, some of whom praise poetry for its alleged generality or universality while others exaggerate its particularity (*VI*, pp. 72–74). One is struck, nevertheless, by how closely the traditional accounts of poetic health, as Wimsatt summarizes them, match Socrates' account of poetry's pathological or perverted relation to the structure of a genuine *technē*. How, then, can poetry's "concrete universality" be a source of both?

Wimsatt's own argument (after his historical survey) begins with the view, which he attributes to Ransom, that

> what distinguishes poetry from scientific or logical discourse is a degree of irrelevant concreteness in descriptive details . . . The irrelevance is a texture of concreteness which does not contribute anything to the argument but is somehow enjoyable or valuable for its own sake, the vehicle of a metaphor which one boards heedless of where it runs, whether crosstown or downtown—just for the ride. (*VI*, p. 76)

But as the joke at the end shows, Wimsatt is dissatisfied with this account, no doubt for the essentially Platonic/Socratic reason that it makes the diversion of interest from object to representation all too obvious. Nor is it clear to Wimsatt how appealing to the sheer irrelevance of detail really manages to distinguish the literary from other forms of discourse involving exemplification.[12] "The fact is," he writes, "that all concrete illustration has about it something of the irrelevant.

An apple falling from a tree illustrates gravity, but apple and tree are irrelevant to the pure theory of gravity." The solution to this dilemma—that is, the dilemma that literary interest begins to look either specially perverse or trivially indistinguishable from any case of being interested in illustrative detail—will be to see that the concrete irrelevance of poetic illustration is in fact a special kind of relevance after all: "It may be that what happens in a poem is that the apple and the tree are somehow made more than usually relevant" (*VI*, p. 76). And this notion of an unusual relevance of detail soon yields a formula that sums up the ontological and epistemological virtues—the complexity, the objectivity and immediacy, the unparaphrasability and hence the irreplaceability—of the literary artifact as conceived by New Criticism: "A literary work of art is a complex of detail . . . , a composition so complicated of human values that its interpretation is dictated by the understanding of it, and so complicated as to seem in the highest degree individual—a concrete universal" (*VI*, p. 77).

Without further explication, the formula is immediately illustrated, and by a reference not to some special property of literary language but, remarkably, to the representation of agency: "We are accustomed to being told, for example, that what makes a character in fiction or drama vital is a certain fullness or rotundity." Wimsatt cites E. M. Forster's distinction between "round" characters and "flat" ones, such as "humours," "types," or "caricatures." According to Forster, the difference lies in the number of ideas or qualities around which the character is constructed, but Wimsatt revises Forster's distinction by suggesting that

> the many traits of the round character . . . are harmonized or unified, and . . . if this is so, then all the traits are chosen by a principle, just as are the traits of the flat character. Yet it cannot be that the difference between the round and flat character is simply numerical; the difference cannot be merely that the presiding principle is illustrated by more examples in the round character. Something further must be supposed—a special interrelation in the traits of the round character.

Wimsatt then offers an example of a "round character" in his sense; unsurprisingly, his example is Falstaff, who has a "vitality of consciousness" and, more important, "the crowning complexity of self-consciousness." "In Falstaff," according to Wimsatt, there is a kind of interrelation among his attributes, his cowardice, his wit, his debauchery, his presumption, that makes them in a special way an organic harmony. He is a rounded character not only in the sense that he is gross (a fact which may have tempted critics to speak of a rounded character) or in the sense that he is a bigger bundle of attributes, stuffed more full, than Bobadil or Ralph Roister Doister; but in the sense that his attributes make a circuit and a connection. A kind of awareness of self (a high and human characteristic), with a pleasure in the fact, is perhaps the central principle which instead of simplifying the attributes gives each one a special function in the whole, a double or reflex value. Falstaff or such a character of self-conscious "infinite variety" as Cleopatra are concrete universals because they have no class names, only their own proper ones, yet are structures of such precise variety and centrality that each demands a special interpretation in the realm of human values. (*VI,* pp. 78–79)[13]

This passage reveals clearly enough why Wimsatt thinks of round characters as examples of concreteness. The more a character is represented as self-conscious, the harder it becomes to see that character as exemplifying a general *type* of character (and thus as representing a general *type* of person). One is reminded of Nelson Goodman's principle that "a symbol that denotes itself also exemplifies itself, is both denoted and exemplified by itself";[14] the more Falstaff seems to refer to himself, the more the type he exemplifies seems to contain only him.

But there is a limit to any fictional character's concreteness, if concreteness is understood in these terms, since nearly all the "attributes" to which Falstaff refers, when he refers to himself, are shared by numerous other characters as well. Many besides Falstaff are gross, cowardly, witty, and/or debauched; in that sense, Falstaff exemplifies many properties that are also exemplified by other characters, which is just another way of saying that he is the product of many literary conventions. What difference does it make whether Falstaff is represented as referring to his "own" attributes, when those attributes themselves are widely shared? How does the mere fact of a character's self-reference, or the mere fiction of a character's self-consciousness, make a multiplicity of attributes more "concrete" than a singularity of attributes? Is the sentence "This sentence is in English" in any interesting way more concrete, or a better fusion of concreteness and universality, than the sentence "*That* sentence is in French"? As this aptly trivial case reveals, a self-referential symbol is really no more "concrete" than any other case of indexicality. Similarly, a round character who is made to refer to his own attributes, no matter how various, is not for that reason any more concrete than a character who is made to refer to anything else. How, then, has Wimsatt really gotten beyond Forster's notion that what distinguishes a round character from a flat one is merely an increase in the number of its attributes?

It is not self-reference, then, that makes a literary symbol like Falstaff or Cleopatra seem concrete, or in a special way concretely universal. So what does? One possible answer is suggested by Wimsatt when he remarks in passing that the "central principle" of Falstaff's roundness is an "awareness of self," together with "a *pleasure* in the fact." Perhaps it is not self-reference as such but the *experience* that accompanies it, the special coincidence of awareness and pleasure, that creates the impression that the various typical attributes Falstaff both possesses and refers to are here united in a unique and therefore irreplaceable or untranslatable mixture.

Yet Falstaff's and Cleopatra's awareness and pleasure are of course fictions—two more fictive properties, in themselves no more or less concrete than grossness or cowardice or "infinite variety." What they lack is precisely what makes nonfictive instances of awareness and pleasure genuinely concrete—quite simply, the fact of embodiment. Real awareness, real pleasure, are concrete precisely because they are not just concepts but are embodied experiences, which in this context is only to say that, unlike concepts, they are inseparably bound to the spatial and temporal conditions of the bodies in which they occur. One way to imagine the existence of a concrete universal in Wimsatt's sense might consequently be to treat a symbol as if it could itself have—or perhaps as if it could *be*—an experience, which would amount to treating it as if it could have or be a body.

After all, a mere *conjunction* of symbol and experience in someone's consciousness—for instance, someone's thinking about Falstaff and experiencing pleasure—would not amount to a fusion of concreteness and universality, since it would do nothing at all to make the symbol's meaning more concrete or the embodied experience more universal. There would be no such thing as a special literary "meaning"; instead, we would be left with an arbitrary transfer of interest from the objects ostensibly represented by the work to the bodies of the various agents engaged in its production and reception. And in that case, the Pla-

tonic/Socratic suspicion about literary discourse would seem to be con-
firmed. For Plato's Socrates, the literary is precisely a discourse in
which meaning is continually displaced by embodied experience,
which is what accounts, according to Socrates, for its affinities with
debilitating emotion, the passions of the rabble, and women. We saw
earlier the connection in *Ion* between the concreteness of literary
agency and the contagion of emotion, specifically of emotions that can
be read with ease on the surface of the rhapsode's or the spectators'
bodies. Well-known passages elsewhere make the connection still more
obvious. Poetic imitation, Socrates argues in *The Republic,* appeals to
our lower faculties, faculties rendered unreliable precisely by their
dependence on bodily location. For instance, imitation is associated
with sight, which, unlike our faculties of measuring and calculating,
alters the magnitude of objects according to their relative nearness to
or distance from the body that sees them (X.602c-603b). The emotions easiest to imitate and hence communicate are the ones most visible, most obviously embodied, the ones that suit a "lachrymose and
fitful temper," that appeal to the "irrational, useless, and cowardly"
part of our nature; not the manly part—the power of self-control on
which we pride ourselves—but "the part of a woman" (X.603e-605e).
In assimilating poetic concreteness to the grossness of Falstaff and the
fitful multiplicity of Cleopatra, Wimsatt thus verges on endorsing Socrates' diagnosis of the literary pathology. Indeed, this Platonic/Socratic
subtext makes clear what was perhaps already obvious, the rather grim
aptness of Wimsatt's choice of examples: a fat man and a woman, traditional emblems of excessive embodiment.[15]

To shift the terms of Socrates' attack on the literary in the direction of his own defense of it, Wimsatt needs, once again, to treat the
literary symbol as itself in some sense embodied, so that what looks
to Plato's Socrates like an irrational turn from meaning to experience
will count instead as a kind of powerfully (and appropriately) fixed
meaning. He attempts this by means of an unannounced return to
the Longinian mutuality of reference described at the beginning of
this chapter. Longinus, equating the sublimity of Homer's text with
the greatness of Homer himself, left us uncertain whether he was
suggesting only that these two kinds of greatness were *similar,* or
that Homer's greatness was what *explained* the greatness of his text,
or finally that Homer's greatness was the actual *content* of his text,
that is, the object to which his text actually referred. None of these

possibilities, by itself, is especially interesting; even the third possibility is by itself no less trivial than any other case of self-reference, or indeed than any other case of an indexical reference. "This text is really about me, its author," or "what you are reading is an account of the very experience you are having while reading it"—these are referential statements like any other, and, from anything like a Platonic/Socratic perspective, remarkably trivial ones at that. "Instead of *that* body"—say, the imagined body of a god or a hero—"I now direct your attention to *this* one."

What can make the Longinian structure look like more than an arbitrary toggling of referents is the way the objects between which attention switches come to seem mutually implicated. Switching from Ajax to Homer, one sees the passions of Ajax inscribed on Homer's face, and yet one was directed to Homer in the first place by a recognition that Homer's own greatness was what his depiction of Ajax was really about. The switching of interest from one object to the other thus begins to look like a response to a referential tendency internal to each object. And essentially the same structure emerges in Wimsatt's refashioning of the Platonic/Socratic turn from universal meaning to concrete experience. It isn't enough that a literary symbol *refer* to the experience that accompanies its reception; that would merely add one more to the numerous objects to which a literary symbol, or any symbol, can refer. The crucial step is to reverse the referential relation by treating the experience itself as in some sense pointing back to the literary symbol that both occasions it and refers to it. While this step is already present in the way Wimsatt slips the notion of pleasure into his account of Falstaff's self-consciousness, its logic is more amply revealed when Wimsatt turns from character to what he considers the most important example of concrete universality, namely, metaphor. Even here, however, the appeal to experience is never explicitly acknowledged; Wimsatt's terminology remains resolutely conceptual:

> Even the simplest form of metaphor or simile ("My love is like a red, red rose") presents us with a special and creative, in fact a concrete, kind of abstraction different from that of science. For behind a metaphor lies a resemblance between two classes, and hence a more general third class. This class is unnamed and most likely remains unnamed and is apprehended only through the metaphor. It is a new conception for which there is no other expression.

The previous chapter already explored the widespread claim that a metaphor can be said to express a "new conception," and I will not return to that issue here. In the present context, it is enough to notice how the very next sentence reveals that the "new conception" for which there is no other expression is not in fact a conception at all but an experience. The example is also, as it happens, amazingly Longinian:

> Keats discovering Homer is like a traveler in the realms of gold, like an astronomer who discovers a planet, like Cortez gazing at the Pacific. The title of the sonnet, "On First Looking into Chapman's Homer," seems to furnish not so much the subject of the poem as a fourth member of a central metaphor, the real subject of the poem being an abstraction, a certain kind of thrill in discovering, for which there is no other name and no other description, only the four members of the metaphor pointing, as to the center of their pattern. The point of the poem seems to lie outside both vehicle and tenor. (VI, pp. 79–80)

Why, one wants to ask, isn't "thrill in discovering" a sufficient name for what the four members of the metaphor point to? And why does this unnameable abstraction lie simultaneously at the center of the pattern and altogether outside it? The answer emerges as soon as one recognizes that the only thrill inseparable from this particular configuration of metaphors is the thrill produced by encountering this particular configuration of metaphors, a thrill—that is, an experience—whose contours are uniquely defined by the particular cognitive and emotive effects of these metaphors and the temporal order in which they succeed each other.[16] Keats's sonnet, on what I am taking to be Wimsatt's implicit account here, is not just about an experience but about an experience that is shaped by, and can thus be read as referring to, the poem that refers to it, just as Homer's description of Ajax, according to Longinus, is not just about Homer but about Homer specifically insofar as Homer reflects and refers to his description of Ajax. The fact that in one case the experience is located in the poet, while in another case it is located in the reader,[17] is less important than the fact that in both cases what takes place is a transfer of interest from a poem's semantic content to an experience that can in turn be read as pointing back to the "center" of the poem itself. (One effect of the Longinian account is to make poet and reader interchangeable anyway—since both are interchangeably possessed by an excellence equally imputed to the composition itself.)[18] The result, in any case, is a (potentially) permanent oscillation of interest between the abstract meanings of the text and one or another subject of concrete experience, an oscillation conceived as fusing or reconciling the universality of language and the particularity of embodiment.

Part of what makes it possible for Wimsatt to treat the oscillation of literary interest as if it were a uniqueness of literary cognition is the way he avoids explicit reference to the reader whose pleasure in Falstaff or whose thrill in discovery implicitly underwrites the concreteness of Wimsatt's examples. The reader's role is rendered more explicit, however, in a passage by Wimsatt's predecessor I. A. Richards, who is rather less discreet than Wimsatt in the way he mobilizes the possibilities of Longinian oscillation. Richards is defending Coleridge's distinction between imagination and fancy, a distinction that, along with several other Coleridgean notions, clearly anticipates the New Critical account of the concrete universal. He begins with Coleridge's remark on a couplet from Shakespeare's *Venus and Adonis* describing Adonis's flight. Here is the couplet:

> Look! how a bright star shooteth from the sky
> So glides he in the night from Venus' eye.

And here is Coleridge's comment:

> How many images and feelings are here brought together without effort and without discord—the beauty of Adonis—the rapidity of his flight—the yearning yet helplessness of the enamoured gazer—and a shadowy ideal character thrown over the whole.[19]

Like Wimsatt starting with Forster, Richards begins with what seems to be Coleridge's obvious, if not his only, point here, the sheer multiplicity of connections: "The more the image is followed up, the more links of relevance between the units are discovered." But Richards's next sentence begins to shift our attention almost imperceptibly to agents unmentioned in Coleridge's comment; the shift is accomplished by means of a Longinian analogy between agents located inside and outside the poem:

> As Adonis to Venus, so these lines *to the reader* [my emphasis] seem to linger in the eye like the after-images that make the trail of the meteor. Here Shakespeare is realizing, and making the

reader realize—not by any intensity of effort, but by the fulness and self-completing growth of the response—Adonis' flight as it was to Venus, and the sense of loss, of increased darkness, that invades her.

The appeal to the poet's activity of "realization," an activity imitated by the reader, who *also* imitates the putative experience of Venus, is temporarily supplanted by a semantic analysis of the meanings and interconnections of the couplet's terms:

The separable meanings of each word, *Look!* (our surprise at the meteor, hers at his flight), *star* (a light-giver, an influence, a remote and uncontrollable thing) *shooteth* (the sudden, irremediable, portentous fall or death of what had been a guide, a destiny), *the sky* (the source of light and now of ruin), *glides* (not rapidity only, but fatal ease too), *in the night* (the darkness of the scene and of Venus' world now)—all these separable meanings are here brought into one.

Brought into one, that is, by the unfolding process of the reader's response, as the rest of the paragraph again makes explicit:

And as they come together, as the reader's mind finds cross-connexion after cross-connexion between them, he seems, in becoming more aware of them, to be discovering not only Shakespeare's meaning, but something which he, the reader, is himself making. His understanding of Shakespeare is sanctioned by his own activity in it. As Coleridge says, "You feel him to be a poet, inasmuch as for a time he has made you one—an active creative being."[20]

The reader discovers not only Shakespeare's meaning, but something the reader herself is making; just as, for Longinus, our soul "takes a proud flight, and is filled with joy and vaunting, as though it had itself produced what it has heard." What there thou seest, fair creature, is thyself; or more exactly in the present case, what there thou seest is thy seeing, since, in the terms of Richards's reading, the eye that watches the imagined meteor is both imaged by, and an image of, the eye that watches the flight of Adonis.

My interest is not, however, in the narcissism of this pattern, except insofar as the evocation of narcissism turns out to be, paradoxically, a way of saving the literary from its Platonic/Socratic trivialization. For the narcissism in Richards's account is not itself the object of literary interest but a means of involving the reader's own concrete agency in the multiplicity of the couplet's meanings. What the turn to the reader establishes, for Richards, is not primarily that the poem is about the self but that, in being about the self, it is about something that already contains a reference to the poem that also seems to refer to *it*. These formulas may sound complicated, but they merely paraphrase the logic of Richards's reading; the reader referred to by Shakespeare and by the figure of Venus is discovered to be imitating Shakespeare's activity, just as she is seen to be looking through Venus's eye. Treated both as the object and as the reflection of the couplet's numerous semantic operations, the reader's own experience functions as the pivotal term in an oscillation between meaning and agency that lets these phenomena seem identical.

But why? What is the point of imagining that, at least in especially salient instances of literary representation, the universality of meaning and the concreteness of embodied agency can achieve, or at least approach, identity? Recall the question with which this chapter began—the Socratic question, as it turned out: What does it mean to be more interested in a representation than in what it represents—more interested in a story than in what the story is about, in a poem than in what it imitates, in a symbol than in what the symbol ostensibly refers to? For Plato's Socrates, what it means is a perverse short-circuiting of the ordinary teleology of reference. It is as if one forgot the business of language, ceased to understand it in fact, and lapsed into a pointless admiration of whatever body was doing the talking. Only, it may seem, if meaning itself can be made properly concrete, properly embodied, can the fixing of literary interest in the literary artifact look like more than a parasitic absorption of what should, on any ethical or political or indeed any cognitive account of literary interest, remain an interest in what the artifact refers to outside itself. But if the gap between meaning and embodiment cannot be closed, if the impression that it *is* closed depends on mistaking an oscillation of interest for a conceptual fusion, then one may seem to be left with the question Wimsatt himself posed, and the answer he gave, the year after he wrote "The Concrete Universal": "What then is an adequately serious view of poetry? I submit that this has always been, and remains, difficult if not impossible to define with any rigor" (*VI*, p. 279).

Imagination

On the interpretation I have been developing, Wimsatt's attempt in "The Concrete Universal" to explain the uniqueness of the literary in terms of a special kind of conceptual content was implicitly a response to the Platonic/Socratic charge that literary discourse is either irrational or empty—or, more accurately, both. Yet the argument in the previous section has suggested that Wimsatt's account was complicated, at least according to his own ostensible criteria in this essay, by its evident reliance on affective (not conceptual) notions like pleasure and interest. Nor could Wimsatt embrace, at least overtly, the Longinian option of celebrating the affective power generated by a shifting of attention between poem and object, poet and character, spectacle and spectator, language and body. Does the affective turn in "The Concrete Universal," then, merely signal the ironic demise of Wimsatt's answer to Socrates? If so, then the only answer to Socrates may indeed be the Longinian one, as Wimsatt himself may have been suggesting in the remark I quoted at the end of the previous section. Perhaps, however, there is more to be said about the affective turn than could be said on the basis of Wimsatt's own rather abrupt and surreptitious enactment of it. At least that is the possibility I now propose to explore, by looking more closely at the interaction between signification and experience that constitutes what Wimsatt calls "the concrete universal."

One way to isolate the features of this kind of interaction is by noticing what takes place when a sign is converted into a concrete image. The problem in such cases is "to show how the sign serves to *motivate* the image, how the former includes the latter in a new synthesis."[21] I quote from an extremely suggestive treatment of this problem by Jean-Paul Sartre, who also provides his own example of an effect that seems closely related to what Wimsatt, following Forster, seems to be getting at in the notion of "round" characterization:

> The whimsical Franconay is "doing some impersonations" on the stage of the music hall; I recognize the artist she is imitating: it is Maurice Chevalier. I recognize the imitation: "It is really he," or: "It is poor." What is going on in my consciousness?
>
> The artist appears. She wears a straw hat; she protrudes the lower lip, she bends her head forward. I cease to perceive, I *read,* that is, I

make a significant synthesis. The straw hat is at first a simple sign, just as the cap and the silk kerchief of the real singer are signs that he is about to sing an apache song. That is to say, that at first I do not see the hat of Chevalier *through* the straw hat, but the hat of the mimic refers to Chevalier, as the cap refers to the "apache sphere." To decipher the signs is to produce the concept "Chevalier." (*POI,* pp. 34, 36–37)

The first step in this process is thus a translation of the "material" of Franconay's appearance into a sign (or a cluster of signs) signifying Chevalier. The fact that the material to a certain extent resists such translation—"the impersonator is small, stout, and brunette; a woman who is imitating a man"—indicates, for Sartre, "the essential role of signs: they must clarify and guide consciousness" (*POI,* p. 36). At this point Sartre might seem to be merely recapitulating the Platonic/Socratic account, with its sharp separation of materiality and meaning, as well as its tendency to identify materiality specifically with female embodiment. And indeed it is hard not to avoid the conclusion that the choice of the example (a woman imitating a man) is guided, as was Wimsatt's mention of Cleopatra, by the lingering force of something like the Platonic/Socratic ideology.[22] Nevertheless, what mainly interests Sartre in this account is not the transition from materiality to signification but rather a second transition that essentially reverses the first one:

> To decipher the signs is to produce the concept "Chevalier." At the same time I am making the judgment: "she is imitating Chevalier." With this judgment the structure of consciousness is transformed. The theme, now, is Chevalier. By its central intention, the consciousness is imaginative, it is a question of realizing my knowledge in the intuitive material furnished me. (*POI,* p. 37)

In other words, the *knowledge* of what Franconay is doing is provided by my correctly interpreting certain signs (straw hat, protruding lip, and so forth) as signifying Chevalier. Consciousness becomes imaginative—signification becomes imaginative experience—when I manage to "realize" this knowledge. But what is the nature of such realization? It isn't as if I am suddenly able to map Franconay's features against those of Chevalier: "It is not a question of constructing a perfect *analogue* of the body of Chevalier with the body of the impersonator Franconay. I use but a few of the elements that were functioning just now as signs" (*POI*, p. 38). What, then, makes the difference between knowledge and "realized" knowledge? The answer, according to Sartre, is "affectivity":

> We can now understand the role of feeling in the consciousness of imitation. When I see Maurice Chevalier the perception involves a certain affective reaction. This feeling projects on the face of Maurice Chevalier a certain indefinable quality which we might call his "meaning." In the consciousness of imitation this affective reaction is awakened by the intentioned knowledge and becomes incorporated into the intentional synthesis from the very beginning of the signs and the intuitive realization. The affective sense of Chevalier's face will appear correlatively on the face of Franconay. It is this affective meaning which brings about the synthetic union of the various signs, which animates their frozen barrenness, which gives them life and a certain density. (*POI*, p. 39)

Sartre's explanation of imitation as involving a transfer of affect from one agent to another—and especially his singling out facial visibility as the means of transfer—may remind us of the scandal of mimetic contagion at the heart of Socrates' attack on the rhapsode Ion, who thus turns out to be a distant precursor of Sartre's Franconay. And in fact, Sartre comes strikingly close to Socrates' argument when he concludes his account of Franconay/Chevalier by remarking that "the relationship of the object to the material of the imitation is here one of *possession*. The absent Maurice Chevalier chose the body of a woman to make his appearance" (*POI*, p. 40). But the precise mode of Chevalier's affective "presence" remains to be clarified.

What exactly takes place when one ceases merely to recognize Franconay's performance as signifying "the concept 'Chevalier' " and begins to experience the affective presence of Chevalier? What is the difference between decoding Franconay's performance as a sign of Chevalier and seeing Chevalier *in* that performance? One important difference is signaled by the fact that I could understand the semantic content of Franconay's performance without actually seeing the performance itself. For instance, someone else might tell me what Franconay did and wore and explain that her apparel and gestures were intended to signify the concept "Chevalier." But I could only experience the relevant feeling—I could only see Chevalier *in* the performance—by seeing the actual performance. The duration and intensity of this imaginative experience would depend not only on Franconay's skill in stimulating it but on such factors as the duration of my exposure to Franconay's performance and my location relative to the stage.[23] When I "see" Chevalier, I see him here and now, in this very experience. In short, one's experience of Chevalier's presence, unlike one's understanding of the concept "Chevalier," is bound essentially to the particular conditions under which one comes to have it.

There is nothing very surprising about this way of distinguishing concept and experience. A similar point is sometimes made in connection with Wittgenstein's example of a picture that can be seen two ways: as a duck facing left or a rabbit facing right.[24] I can understand the conceptual content of the picture—I can know that it is intended to be a picture of both a duck and a rabbit—whether or not I am looking at it, and even, presumably, whether or not I find myself capable of experiencing the desired oscillation when I *do* look at it.[25]

To explain the particularity of my experience in this way is not, however, to explain what my experience is an experience *of.* After all, *every* perceptual experience is bound to the viewer's location and capacities.[26] Seeing Franconay herself (as opposed to knowing that someone is Franconay) depends just as much on the location and capacities of the viewer as seeing Chevalier in Franconay's performance. What makes the latter special, on Sartre's account, is its peculiar dependence on affect. This feature of Sartre's analysis is helpfully elaborated by Mary Warnock, who gives the following account of what is involved in forming a mental image of an absent scene:

> The crucial part of knowing that we have succeeded in imagining the scene is that, besides its visual appearance, we should also create, or revive, in ourselves some of the affective aspects of the scene, and feel in ourselves some of the emotions which the scene would produce in us if it were there in reality. In the case of *deliberately* imagining a scene this aspect of it may be the most important of all. We may claim to *be* imagining, let us say, the nave of Winchester cathedral, if we have the feeling, vague and hard to characterize though this feeling may be, which we would have if we were in fact standing, let us say, at the west end of the cathedral, looking towards the east.[27]

Applied to the case of Franconay's performance, Warnock's account suggests that I "see" Chevalier in the performance insofar as I experience "some of the affective aspects" and "some of the emotions" that Chevalier would produce in me if he were present "in reality." As War-

nock says, this affective experience can either be revived or created—
that is, the basis of my expectation can be either a memory of what it
was like when I was actually in Chevalier's presence or an imaginary
construction (based, perhaps, on someone's description) of what it
might feel like if I ever *were* in Chevalier's presence. In either case, just
as my experience of seeing Franconay's performance is bound essentially to the conditions under which I have that experience, so the
"Chevalier-feeling"[28] (the aspect of Chevalier that I see when I see Chevalier in the performance) is bound essentially to the real or imagined
spatial-temporal conditions under which I remember or imagine
having had that feeling. And, lest the phrase "bound essentially" give
rise to metaphysical misgivings, the same point can be made somewhat more technically by saying that the intentional content of the
experience involves an indexical reference both to the present situation
and to the situation or situations I remember or imagine.[29]

But how does this account bear on the specifically *literary* problem
of the concrete universal? Here it is not a matter of imaginatively
seeing one person in another's performance but of seeing a person in a
collection of written signs. Nevertheless, I see no reason to alter the
basic terms of the foregoing analysis. Both cases involve the same transition from meaning to experience, from sign to affect. Of course there
are particular differences deriving from the fact that the signifying
medium in the literary case consists of inscriptions, not physical
objects and gestures. But the sense in which an experience remains
indexically bound both to the situation in which it occurs and to the
remembered or imagined situation or situations from which the subject derives the relevant feeling remains constant in the theatrical and
the literary cases.

Perhaps these reflections on the role of affect in all imaginative
experience provide a way of explaining Wimsatt's version of the distinction between a "flat" character and a "round" one. Perhaps we can
translate Wimsatt's distinction into a distinction between characters
we tend to treat as signifying certain concepts and characters whose
descriptions or narrated actions give rise (or are capable of giving rise)
to the kinds of responses we remember or imagine having in the presence of actual people. One trouble with this approach to the notion of
the concrete universal is that the transition to the round character
moves entirely, it seems, in the direction of concreteness; instead of
reconciling universal meaning and particular experience, it simply

substitutes the latter for the former—as was suggested, in fact, by what seemed to occur in Wimsatt's essay.

Mere substitution, however, is too simple a mechanism to account for what goes on in the example of Franconay's performance. To see why this is so, consider what is involved in supposing that my capacity to see Chevalier in Franconay's performance might derive from a remembered experience of being in Chevalier's actual presence. Recall the crucial moment described by Sartre's account: the imaginative experience, as he analyzes it, involves a transition to an experience of Chevalier's affective presence from "the concept 'Chevalier.' " The very expression "the concept 'Chevalier' " initially sounds odd: isn't Chevalier already a particular person, not a concept, even before the transition from reference to feeling? But this odd locution is in fact correct. What may confuse the issue is Sartre's remark, just before introducing the notion of "the concept 'Chevalier,' " that "the hat of the mimic refers to Chevalier" (*POI*, pp. 36–37). To understand what Franconay is up to is not quite to see her hat as referring to a particular body designated Chevalier and located, perhaps, in another part of Paris. It is instead to recognize her hat as a Chevalier-hat—that is, as an example of a certain recognizable *type* of hat. It is also to recognize the mimic herself as *a Chevalier,* an example of the *type* of person that Chevalier has become and, in virtue of this exemplification, a sign of the concept "Chevalier." Other hats and other mimics could serve the same signifying function by likewise becoming examples of the relevant types; nor is there any reason why Chevalier's own hat, and indeed Chevalier himself, when "playing" Chevalier, might not be recognized as signifying in exactly the same way. (Perhaps, reversing Sartre's narrative, Chevalier himself on occasion failed to produce in his audience the Chevalier-feeling and was reduced to serving only as a sign of the concept "Chevalier.")

Chevalier, once again—the Chevalier that Franconay's performance first signifies and then embodies—is not the particular body designated Chevalier but a certain type of embodied look and behavior, a look and behavior with, as Warnock puts it, a certain "style."[30] For that reason it might be possible to acquire a remembered repertoire of Chevalier-situations, in response to which one might have the Chevalier-feeling, without ever seeing the actual body of Chevalier. Suppose, for example, that before witnessing Franconay's performance I have never seen Chevalier himself, even on film—but I have previously seen someone else, another mimic, "do" Chevalier. Then my capacity to see Chevalier in Franconay's performance will be bound indexically to my memory not of the particular man Chevalier (I have no such memory) but of the mimic's performance. In that case—and assuming that I then knew that what I saw on the remembered occasion was someone imitating Chevalier—the affective state I now revive when I imagine Chevalier will be connected not to a previous experience of *seeing* Chevalier but to a previous experience of *imagining* him.

The next step is to notice that this will be true even if I *have* seen an actual performance by the historical Chevalier, since Chevalier himself, as he then existed and acted, will have served only as one possible example of the Chevalier-type. To see Chevalier "in" a performance, then, is only to imagine oneself seeing *another* "Chevalier" in *another* performance. Every such experience of Chevalier-seeing is an experience in which one sees Chevalier imaginatively in a performance that exemplifies the Chevalier-type, which is to say, the character Chevalier. The feeling I revive or create in myself when I see Chevalier in Franconay's performance is thus a feeling I associate with other similar experiences. In general, to succeed in imagining a *type* of object, character, or situation involves producing in oneself the feeling that one would experience if one were in the presence of another example of the same type of object, character, or situation. In any case of "seeing" a character in the cluster of signs that exemplify that character-type and hence signify that character-concept, both my present experience and the remembered or imagined experience to which it refers remain irreducibly inhabited by the generality of the type exemplified, the concept referred to. And yet the type in question is precisely a typical *experience,* involving a typical affective response. That may help to explain why the transition from sign to image, for the spectator of Franconay's performance, was possible in the first place: because the image of Chevalier—that is, the typical Chevalier-experience—already possessed a semantic structure linking a typical affective response to typical signs of the concept "Chevalier."

But now consider what has happened. By spelling out the implications of Sartre's brief mention of "the concept 'Chevalier,' " we have arrived at the notion of a particular feeling experienced on a particular occasion, but a feeling that at the same time possesses the irreducible generality of a concept, since it necessarily involves a reference to other feelings on other occasions (whether those other feelings are remembered or only imagined). We have arrived, in short, at something it apparently does make sense to call a "concrete universal." Have we therefore arrived, at last, at the notion of literary meaning that Wimsatt was after?

In a sense we have, but so far only by sacrificing its literary specificity. For the version of the concrete universal to which Sartre's account has led us turns out to be a characteristic feature of imaginative experience in general. To imagine anything, again on Warnock's version of the Sartrean account, is to "feel in ourselves some of the emotions which the [object] would produce in us if it were there in reality." Even if one is imagining an actual object encountered only once before, one's affective experience involves the irreducibly general or conceptual feature of a necessary reference to another response on another occasion.

And here is a further difficulty: if this principle applies to the experience of imagining a fictional character, it equally applies to the experience of imagining an actual person. When it comes to persons, in fact, the account needs to be pushed one step further. Sartre's example concerned the *imagining* of an absent person, but his account applies equally to the *perception* of persons as such. For persons, in a crucial sense, are *always* absent. To perceive a person is always to perceive a particular body as the present incarnation of an identity that is distributed across a range of particular occasions now absent. (And this remains true of our perception of persons, incidentally, no matter what sort of metaphysical account one gives of personal identity itself.) Thus Franconay is just as much a site of "possession" when we see her *as* Franconay as when we see her as Chevalier.[31]

From this point of view, the trouble with Wimsatt's treatment of a figure like Falstaff may be not that there is no such thing as a concrete universal but that Wimsatt makes the literary version of it seem trivially ordinary; Falstaff's concrete universality comes to seem indistinguishable from the concrete universality already built into our perception of actual persons, as well as our ordinary imaginings of whatever we happen to imagine. One way out of this difficulty might be to suggest that what matters in the case of Falstaff is not, as Wimsatt says, the fact that "his attributes make a circuit and connection" (*VI*, p. 79). On the contrary: his special status may depend on his capacity to evoke a range of figures and situations outside the circuit of an ordinary person's own "personality." Otherwise, his concrete universality would in no way differ from that of anyone else we might find ourselves imagining. What may make Falstaff a peculiarly *literary* instance of concrete universality may be the degree to which the conventionality of his attributes—as well as their formal associations with other features of the texts in which they appear—enables them to evoke a range of characters and situations external to the character "himself." The diversity of what they refer to may actually *prevent* Falstaff's attributes from "making a circuit," and therefore prevent Falstaff himself from lapsing into the status of a (merely) actual person. If this is correct so far, then such diversity of reference may turn out to be, for reasons explored below, what gives Falstaff a peculiarly literary kind of particularity.

Literary Affect

If nothing else, the account of imaginative experience developed in the previous section would seem to warrant a reconsideration of the Platonic/Socratic argument. According to that argument, as I have interpreted it, the degree to which literary representation seemed bound to particular sources of affective power revealed its essential irrationality. What the argument overlooked, however, was the possibility that the very affectivity of literary representation (and to some extent of all imagination) might possess its own kind of generality and hence, in a way, its own kind of rationality. (This possibility may not have been entirely overlooked even in *Ion:* remember the rhapsode's ability to gauge the degree to which his affective states were communicated to his audience.)

To some extent at least, Wimsatt apparently accepted the Platonic identification of affect and irrationality. After all, the "two forms of irresponsibility" (*VI,* p. 5) that he and Beardsley diagnosed—the Intentional and the Affective Fallacies—were really both *affective* fallacies, since what was "irresponsible" about the Intentional Fallacy was mainly its appeal to the author's "private" feelings and attitudes. At the beginning of "The Affective Fallacy," for instance, Wimsatt and Beardsley describe the two fallacies as both involving an excessive attention to psychology. The only difference is that the Intentional Fallacy tries "to derive the standard of criticism from the psychological *causes* of the poem and ends in biography and relativism," while the Affective Fallacy tries "to derive the standard of criticism from the psychological effects of the poem and ends in impressionism and relativism. The outcome of either Fallacy . . . is that the poem itself, as an object of specifically critical judgment, tends to disappear" (*VI*, p. 21). As "The Intentional Fallacy" had insisted, what keeps the poem visible—and criticism a responsibly "public" enterprise—is the determination of poetic meaning by publicly accessible linguistic norms, and "in general by all that makes a language and culture" (*VI*, p. 10).[32]

This hostility to both the poet's affective input and the reader's affective response is compatible with allowing a certain place for affect in poetry—namely, as an important part of what a poem can be *about*. But the very manner in which they grant affect a central referential or thematic status *within* poetry makes clearer than ever why Wimsatt and Beardsley fail to grasp, at least explicitly, the special relevance of affective experience to the character of literary rationality. Consider, for instance, the following passage, taken from the concluding paragraphs of "The Affective Fallacy":

> Poetry is characteristically a discourse about both emotions and objects, or about the emotive qualities of objects. The emotions correlative to the objects of poetry become a part of the matter dealt with—not communicated to the reader like an infection or disease, not inflicted mechanically like a bullet or knife wound, not administered like a poison, not simply expressed as by expletives or grimaces or rhythms, but presented in their objects and contemplated as a pattern of knowledge. (*VI*, p. 38)

Poetry as such is thus saved from an intrinsic association with affective experience, which becomes merely one of the various things a poem can refer to. In that case, however, what does poetry add to our ordinary knowledge about emotions and our ordinary practices of referring to them? The key term here is obviously *pattern*—not just knowledge, but "a pattern of knowledge." And this leads directly to an unusual account of what it might mean to think of a literary emotion as located within the literary artifact itself, instead of in the reader. A poem, on this account, becomes a kind of Rosetta Stone or translation manual, in which the alignment of objects bearing similar emotive "values" enables one to recover the value of objects whose emotional significance would otherwise be lost over time (for instance, when the waning of monarchy diminishes the horror of regicide):

Poetry is a way of fixing emotions or making them more permanently perceptible when objects have undergone a functional change from culture to culture, or when as simple facts of history they have lost emotive value with loss of immediacy . . . The murder of Duncan by Macbeth [becomes in Shakespeare's play] an act difficult to duplicate in all its immediate adjuncts of treachery, deliberation, and horror of conscience. Set in its galaxy of symbols— the hoarse raven, the thickening light, and the crow making wing, the babe plucked from the breast, the dagger in the air, the ghost, the bloody hands—this ancient murder has become an object of strongly fixed emotive value. (*VI*, p. 38)

That is, we can find out what emotions used to accompany the thought of regicide because regicide has been linked, in Shakespeare's play, with a range of objects whose emotive significance hasn't changed.

The plausible assumption behind this archaeological scenario is that certain objects mentioned in a poem consistently signify certain emotions. Earlier in the essay, Wimsatt and Beardsley offer the following explanation of how such signification works:

It is a well known but nonetheless important truth that there are two kinds of real objects which have emotive quality, the objects which are the reasons for human emotion, and those which by some kind of association suggest either the reasons or the resulting emotion: the thief, the enemy, or the insult that makes us angry, and the hornet that sounds and stings somewhat like ourselves when angry; the murderer or felon, and the crow that kills small birds and animals or feeds on carrion and is black like the night when crimes are committed by men. The arrangement by which these two kinds of emotive meaning are brought together in a juncture characteristic of poetry is, roughly speaking, the simile, the metaphor, and the various less clearly defined forms of association. (*VI*, p. 36)

On this view, it would seem to be possible to know what emotion an object is supposed to signify without oneself experiencing anything like the emotion in question. One merely has to know that certain objects (properly? typically?) either give rise to certain emotions or else remind people of objects that give rise to those emotions. The whole point of "The Affective Fallacy" is, in fact, to insist on the possibility of such knowledge, and thus to deny that emotive meaning involves an irrational (Ion-like) transfer of affect from poem to reader.

But there remains a certain ambiguity as to the precise nature of the "knowledge" that one is supposed be after here. For one thing, the connections between objects and emotions would seem to be rather looser than is implied by the image of "fixing" an object's emotive value by setting it in its "galaxy of symbols." The connections in question are plainly not, on Wimsatt's and Beardsley's own account, semantic connections in any strict sense; they are rather connections of inference ("the *reasons* for human emotion") and of association. Moreover, it seems puzzling to say that Duncan's murder "has become an object of strongly fixed emotive *value.*" All that has been fixed, if Wimsatt and Beardsley are right, is the possibility of finding out what emotive value regicide *used* to have. We can find this out because babes and crows and so forth continue to have (by hypothesis, at least) something like the same emotive value they had when Shakespeare wrote the play. But why should our capacity to find out what emotions regicide induced *back then* have anything to do with the value we assign it *now?* Or is the knowledge we acquire somehow necessarily connected, after all, to our present affective response? Is that what makes it the kind of knowledge that can "fix" emotive value? But what kind of knowledge, exactly, is that?

A related ambiguity emerges earlier in the essay when Wimsatt and Beardsley focus on the status of emotion in what we would now recognize as the practice of New Critical explication:

> The more specific the account of the emotion induced by a poem, the more nearly it will be an account of the reasons for emotion, the poem itself, and the more reliable it will be as an account of what the poem is likely to induce in other—sufficiently informed—readers. It will in fact supply the kind of information which will enable readers to respond to the poem. (*VI,* p. 34)

Here the utility of criticism clearly goes beyond (though it still includes) its role in enabling the reader to contemplate a pattern of knowledge. For the knowledge one is ultimately after is knowledge that will enable the right emotive response in readers who acquire it. It is knowledge of "the reasons for emotion," that is, reasons for the emotion "induced by [the] poem" in question. But then what are the emotions induced by the poem? How does one find out what those are? Not by referring to some record of *past* responses, a course of inquiry that Wimsatt and Beardsley explicitly reject (*VI,* pp. 27–28). And not by observing the response that people generally tend to have, since there would then be no need to inform them of it.

We are forced to conclude that a critic—even one "whose formulations," as Wimsatt and Beardsley put it, "lean to the cognitive" and not "to the emotive" (*VI*, p. 34)—can only identify the "reasons for emotion," and thus decode the semantic links between object and emotion, after noticing what emotions the poem "induces" in the critic herself. The entire critical process would seem, then, to have something like the following structure. The critic first reads the poem and identifies the objects it refers to. This knowledge somehow "induces" emotions appropriate to those objects, in something like the way the signs employed by Franconay's performance eventually, in Sartre's account, induced the "affectivity" of Chevalier. The critic then reverses the process, specifying the semantic information that induced the experience. And this information in turn enables another reader to undergo the same transition from semantic understanding to affective experience.

What does all this amount to, however, except a somewhat roundabout return to the Platonic/Socratic scandal of a mere transfer of affect from one agent to another? The only thing added, so far, by the New Critical account is the particular mechanism of exchange, namely the critic's semantic analysis. If anything, the problem would seem to be exacerbated by the perversion, from a Platonic/Socratic perspective, of a rational skill into one more instrument of affective contagion.

The trouble with the New Critical account is not, however, simply that it fails in its attempt to subordinate affect to semantic structure. It also fails to see what the interaction of semantic structure and affect implies about the nature of affect, and especially of literary affect. For the "objects" by which the emotions are suggested must be *types* of objects or occasions, not particular remembered ones. Otherwise it would make no sense to expect the objects constituting the critic's "reasons for emotion" to constitute similar reasons for the reader informed by the critic's account, unless one supposed that they shared the same particular memories. But if the emotion can be communicated only insofar as it is associated with a more or less general *type* of object, then the experience of such an emotion necessarily involves a reference to a *range* of possible occasions of experiencing it.

Thus affective experience, if it is communicable at all in the way presupposed by the cognitivist account, must have a built-in generality that already complicates any stark opposition between private emotion and public knowledge. The objects (situations, and so forth) with which emotions are associated are general *types* of objects, and the emotional responses must have a similar typicality, since otherwise a reader who understood the type of object referred to would not even be *likely* (except by chance) to share the appropriate response. Emotions, consequently, don't need to be inserted into a semantic structure in order to be rescued from irrational particularity; they already *have* a semantic structure in virtue of their dependence on, and irreducible reference to, what Ronald de Sousa has recently called "paradigm scenarios." On de Sousa's hypothesis,

> We are made familiar with the vocabulary of emotion by association with *paradigm scenarios*. These are drawn first from our daily life as small children and later reinforced by the stories, art, and culture to which we are exposed. Later still, in literate cultures, they are supplemented and refined by literature. Paradigm scenarios involve two aspects: first, a situation type providing the characteristic *objects* of the specific emotion-type . . . and second, a set of characteristic or "normal" *responses* to the situation, where normality is first a biological matter and then very quickly becomes a cultural one.[33]

So far there is nothing especially literary about de Sousa's account of emotion, which in fact applies to (communicable) emotion in general. Of course we can immediately move de Sousa's account closer to the specifically literary by saying (and this is not a trivial addition) that literary "scenarios" conjoin emotion-types and object-types not only with each other but also with appropriate *linguistic* expressions. But the mere addition of linguistic associations to emotive ones does not yet explain how paradigm scenarios are, as de Sousa puts it, "supplemented and refined by literature."

To get at the kind of generality that is peculiar to *literary* emotions, consider, once again, the case of Duncan's murder as inserted into the semantic network (the "galaxy of symbols") of Shakespeare's play. According to Wimsatt and Beardsley, the play "fixes" the murder's "emotive value." It does so by the way its language and its represented actions associate one object or (in de Sousa's more exact terminology) one object-type—a certain type of murder—with a range of other object-types, each possessing its own emotive value. But why suppose that its association with *other* object-types "fixes" an object-type's emotive value? Why not say that such association precisely *un*fixes the object-type's value—or affixes a *new* value—by altering the range of responses with which this type of murder is associated?

In de Sousa's terms, we can suggest that Duncan's murder had, in the first place, whatever emotive value it had because it exemplified an object-type (regicide) that could be seen as fitting into a certain paradigm scenario, or more likely a range of such scenarios, no doubt peculiar to a certain type of monarchic society. Those scenarios, which pre-existed the play, presumably connected various acts of betrayal, crimes against fathers, and violations of the divine order with certain appropriate responses. But then what happened, on this account, when Duncan's murder was connected, by the particular form of the play's represented actions and its verbal details, with a collection of *other* object-types? What happened when it became not just regicide but regicide at night, by means of a dagger, resulting in bloody hands, and, in its assault on a sleeping and therefore innocent victim, characterized by the same negation of pity that would be shown by someone's plucking a babe from a breast? Presumably each of these other object-types must have carried with it its own emotive paradigm scenarios, with which Duncan's murder was now associated. So instead of securing the murder's connection to its original paradigm scenario (and thus "fixing" its emotive value), its identification with these other object-types must now have associated it with a collection of new scenarios, so that it became a potential occasion of the responses already linked to those object-types in *their* respective paradigm scenarios. But of course the same thing was also happening to the other object-types, each of which was now associated with the scenarios suggested by (this example of) regicide, as well as the scenarios suggested by all the other object-types.[34]

The result can only have been the production, for each emotive object, of a new composite paradigm scenario, one involving a complex realignment of previously existing object-types and response-types. This is not, of course, to suppose that anyone ever experienced all the relevant responses, or ever had all the relevant objects "in mind." Not even the simplest paradigm scenarios can ever be present in anyone's consciousness, since, for one thing, every scenario must involve a reference to the open set of objects possibly exemplifying the relevant object-types. Despite the particularizing effect of its insertion into the composite, each scenario retains an irreducible typicality. (Otherwise it wouldn't be paradigmatic.) Still, the production of a new composite scenario changes the emotive value of each of the component object-types. Regicide now becomes part of a composite object-type that also contains thickening light, rooky woods, and so on—and not just these object-types but the particular verbal expressions with which the play connects them. It derives a new emotive value from its association with (and hence its at least potential capacity to evoke) each of the range of paradigm scenarios conjoined, for the first time, by this new network of associations. Nor is it likely to acquire anything like the same emotive value outside its position within this network. (The murder as situated in the play becomes, as Wimsatt and Beardsley say, "difficult to reproduce in all its immediate adjuncts.") Literary emotions thus turn out to have somewhat peculiar semantic structures. If such emotions are unusually comprehensive in the range of objects and responses they embrace, they are also unusually specialized in their dependence on highly particular conjunctions of previously independent scenarios.

Thus it seems that the special emotive consequence of literary representation is not, as Wimsatt and Beardsley seem to argue, the production of an unusually stable or objective *knowledge* of previously existing emotions. Rather, it is the *transformation* of those emotions. Emotions are liable to transformation in this way because they have semantic or quasi-semantic structures (the "paradigm scenarios" in which they are linked, by inference and association, to their appropriate object-types), structures that are necessarily altered by their affiliation with other such structures. Ironically, then, one reason emotions cannot be used to underwrite the claims of literature as a special form of knowledge is that emotions themselves are *not* irrational particulars. Emotions themselves possess an irreducible typicality. In this sense, they turn out to have at least a quasi-rationality—though this very "rationality" is also a source of instability, since it depends, once again, on inferential and associative relations that are bound to be affected when a given emotive object-type is inserted into a new associative context. From this perspective, the trouble with Wimsatt and Beardsley's version of New Criticism was not that it was too formalist (too hostile to psychological particularity) but that it didn't carry its formalism far enough.

Apparently, then, the notion of the concrete universal, as an account of the uniqueness of literary representation, can be defended after all, once one recognizes the precise sense in which a literary structure effects a particularizing conjunction of the scenarios that give emotions and objects their typical relations. Before settling on such a formula, however, it is important to notice that emotive value isn't the only kind of value that is likely to change when an object is inserted into a new associative context. Ethical scenarios, linking object-types and types of *ethical* response, are presumably also subject to transformation in this way (assuming that such scenarios can in fact be separated from emotive ones). But so, indeed, are any *thoughts* that are typically associated with a given object-type. Once one sees that there is nothing uniquely particular or irrational about emotive paradigm scenarios, it becomes unclear why emotive responses should be given any special role at all in the definition of a work's concrete universality. And at that point, it becomes hard to see, finally, what more there is to say about concrete universality beyond the observation that *typical* responses of all kinds are likely to be given a new and highly *particular* content when their objects are brought into new associations.

And where, exactly, does that leave us? What answer does it provide to the charges of literary parasitism and uselessness with which this chapter began? We may have answered the Platonic/Socratic charge of sheer irrationality. But how far, after all, have we really progressed beyond Wimsatt's crypto-Longinian formula—that the aesthetic symbol "absorbs the interest of its referents into itself and contains it in an impractical stasis"? At most we can now revise the formula along something like the following lines: a literary representation particularizes the emotive (and other) values of its referents by inserting those referents into new composite scenarios whose composition is in various ways shaped by the particular linguistic and narrative structures of the representation itself.[35] The direction of literary interest, defined in these terms, would seem to remain fundamentally centripetal. At least it is not obvious, so far, what literary values—linked as they are to such highly specific structures—could be said to contribute to any of our projects outside the production and consumption of literature itself.

4

Literary Value

The Question

This chapter attempts to answer a question implicit throughout the previous one and raised explicitly at the end of it. The question is worth stating at the outset in its crudest form, if only to display its obvious absurdity when so stated: What good is reading literature? The absurdity lies in the apparent assumption that it might be possible to identify the single overriding purpose or benefit of a massive, multifarious, and profoundly unstable institution. (And there are really two institutions, or two *sets* of institutions and practices, involved here: the historically and culturally various institutions and practices of literature itself, and the only slightly more localized institutions and practices of formal literary inquiry.) On the other hand, as soon as one gives up the attempt to arrive at a single answer to the question, it is easy to collect numerous answers of varying degrees of generality. Such answers include, for instance, the satisfaction of curiosity; the garnering of things to quote on the right occasions; the expansion of sympathy; the exploration of new or forgotten social options; the provision of convenient topics for freshman compositions.[1]

I have some sympathy with virtually all the answers I can imagine, as well as with most of the available grounds for distrusting them. But my concern here will be not be to canvass the range of possible reasons for preserving, distributing, and investigating literary texts. I will focus instead on what I take to be a more manageable version of the question mentioned above, a version concerned not with our wildly various relations to literary texts but with the possible ethical and political benefits of literary *interest* as specified in the previous chapter—that is, an interest in representations that construct new compositions of thought and value out of pre-existing relations between words and objects and the responses associated with them (where the "objects" in question are actually types of persons, actions, and situations as well as of "things"). For better or worse, the question in its new version has not lost all its original crudity: What is the benefit, if any, of literary interest, as we have come to define it?

Complexity and Moral Progress

At first, given my account of literary interest, this question might seem to answer itself. If ethical and political action depends on a knowledge of human thought and value, why shouldn't we expect to learn relevant truths from the "new compositions of thought and value" that a literary work constructs "out of existing relations between objects and the responses associated with them"? The trouble with this response is that it isn't obvious why bringing thoughts, values, and objects into new relations, which are therefore unlike the ones they had before, should be thought to enhance our knowledge of these matters as they obtain outside the literary representation. For as we saw at the end of the previous chapter, the novelty of a literary work's "new compositions" lies in the way represented objects acquire new associations, associations they lack outside the composite scenarios into which the work inserts them. Nor is it clear how these associations can be transferred to situations outside the structure of the work in question. On the contrary, the very "concreteness" of the concrete universal turned out to involve the inseparability of literary associations from the peculiar conjunction of scenarios produced by a work itself. That was why the ancient crime of regicide, set in Shakespeare's "galaxy of symbols," could not be said to have retained its original "emotive value." Instead, it had acquired a new and non-transferable value by virtue of its insertion into the play's peculiar network of language and association.

Perhaps, however, the point of literary representation is not so much to display existing emotive (and other) values as to generate *new* possibilities of valuation. Indeed, from one point of view this might seem to be a more important way of developing a knowledge of values than the sort of archaeological recovery Wimsatt and Beardsley seemed to be imagining. Coming to "know" a certain value, after all, means more than simply learning how people have responded to certain situations in the past. One has to develop a sense of what responses are *appropriate* to that situation. And this is not a matter of acquiring information so much as of adding to the repertoire of "paradigm scenarios" that constitute one's axiological dispositions. Here I refer, once again, to the axiological theory of Ronald de Sousa, on whose account of emotive rationality I drew in the discussion of Wimsatt and Beardsley's "Affective Fallacy."[2] And in fact de Sousa himself, drawing on the work of theorists like Iris Murdoch and Martha Nussbaum,[3] affirms the creative role of literary texts in transforming a person's or a culture's scenarios.

Thus the value of literary representation, for de Sousa, is connected to the revisability of the scenarios that, on his theory, constitute the "axiological level of reality" apprehended by our emotions (*RE,* p. 303). According to de Sousa, an emotive paradigm "can always be challenged in the light of a wider range of considerations than are available when the case is viewed in isolation. It can be revised in the light of competing paradigms that are also applicable to the situation at hand." And this possibility of revising a paradigm scenario by confronting it with alternative scenarios yields what de Sousa calls a "principle of emotional continence": "Let your emotions be appropriate to the widest possible range of available scenarios." To illustrate his principle, de Sousa gives "a somewhat politically charged example":

> How do you feel about prostitution? The answer will depend on the model to which—emotionally—you assimilate it: Is it wage labor? . . . It it free-enterprise independent business? Oppression of women? Oppression of men? Therapy? Or theater? A mature emotional reaction to prostitution, according to [the principle of emotional continence], is one that is tested against all these potentially applicable scenarios. (*RE,* p. 187)

Such testing of one scenario against others underlies "the attempt to restructure one's emotions by 'consciousness raising.' " Indeed, according to de Sousa, "moral progress is often a matter of rising above" mere moral principles "by getting a more adequate feel for a certain situation in all its ramifications, by viewing it as a complex scenario." For "a moral principle is bound to construe any situation to which it is applied simplistically" (*RE,* pp. 187–188).

Although he has not yet, in this passage, referred explicitly to literature, de Sousa has captured an intuition widely shared among philosophers and critics who see literary representation as an unusually powerful vehicle of moral progress. But his way of elaborating the intuition already raises a certain question about it. Notice that de Sousa has just given us *two* accounts of what is involved in revising a paradigm scenario. On the first account, a mature response—and therefore, presumably, a mature scenario—is one that has been "tested" against all the scenarios "potentially applicable" to the same situation. But on the second account, the index of moral maturity is an ability to see the situation itself as a "complex scenario." The first account is perfectly straightforward, as far as it goes; it merely restates the Davidsonian principle that practical rationality involves an attempt to "perform the action judged best on the basis of all available relevant reasons."[4] But the second account treats the assessment of a situation in the light of potentially applicable scenarios as if it involved representing the situation itself *as* a complex scenario. The point is no longer, apparently, to choose among competing scenarios or to correct an existing scenario in the light of alternative possibilities but to treat the competing alternatives as if they were all components of a single larger scenario. The second account hardly follows from the first, if it is even compatible with it. But it is the second account, not the first, that matches the structure of literary representation, insofar as *literary* representation is in any important way distinct from other modes of description, narration, argument, and so on.

The fact that de Sousa has literary composition in mind here is revealed by the example he gives to illustrate his claim that moral progress depends on "rising above principle." The example is Huckleberry Finn, who "refrains from turning in Jim, the fugitive slave," even though doing so violates "every principle of honesty and gratitude known to him" (*RE,* p. 188). Huck's action, however salutary, may seem surprising as an instance of complex moral vision, and de Sousa later makes clear that this action, by itself, does not quite involve the production of a new complex scenario; rather "it conforms to a standard paradigm scenario, dictating something like compassion, but is deviant in including Jim among possible recipients of sympathy" (*RE,* p. 252). In this sense, "a definite modification is brought to the original scenario, but only, as it were, in terms of casting." In contrast to Huck's "first-order" rebellion, however,

> Mark Twain's own consciousness . . . represents a rebellion of a higher logical order: by writing the story itself, Mark Twain consciously sets up a clash between two ways of interpreting the notion of compassion. He urges the substitution of a new scenario for the accepted double standard, according to which people come pre-cast in roles that depend on their race. In doing this, he must of course avail himself of an already existing paradigm scenario— perhaps one deriving from Christian egalitarianism.

The double use of the "casting" metaphor already makes this account somewhat puzzling; if the racist scenario of compassion essentially involves "pre-casting" people in roles that depend on their race, why doesn't Huck's *re*-casting of the scenario already amount to a revision on the same level as Twain's? But the main question raised by de Sousa's reading is whether Twain's moral revisionism lies in his "setting up a clash" between two scenarios or merely in his urging the substitution of one existing scenario (the Christian egalitarian one) for another (the racist one involving pre-casting by race). For there is nothing especially complex (let alone especially literary) about the second of these moves. Presumably *all* moral persuasion, in or out of novels, always involves the substitution of one evaluation for another. The question is whether this aim is necessarily furthered by, or (once again) even compatible with, the construction of a new complex scenario in which an object or situation is inserted into a multiplicity of previously existing scenarios. Why assume that the simultaneous projection of competing scenarios will favor the substitution of one scenario for another, let alone of the right scenario for the wrong one? Of course there is no reason why someone might not still decide which scenario was the right one and act accordingly. But in that case the reason for deciding would have to come from outside the complex scenario itself. Or if it *did* come from within the literary representation, this would only occur insofar as the work contained a simplifying moral principle of the kind whose tyranny literary complexity is supposed to resist.

To put the issue in these terms is to make obvious, if it was not obvious already, the political picture that lies behind the assumed connection between literary complexity and moral progress. For an interest in bringing together conflicting views in a single representational space is a well-known feature of a certain liberal conception of political representation.[5] In particular, it evokes what Hanna Fenichel Pitkin has termed the "descriptive" view of representation.[6] According to this view, as Pitkin analyzes it, "What matters is being present, being heard; that is representation." Thus Pitkin cites John Stuart Mill's remark that a representative body is " 'an arena' in which each opinion in the nation 'can produce itself in full light.' "[7] But the weakness of this theory, paralleling the weakness of de Sousa's account of "complex scenarios," is that it leaves unclear exactly how the mere "giving of information about constituents' views" is supposed to result in appropriate action, which in the political case involves "acting for, or on behalf of, others." This means, again in the political case, that descriptive theory "has no room for the creative activities of a representative legislature, the forging of consensus, the formulating of policy, the activity we roughly designate by 'governing.' "[8]

And there is a further parallel between the political and literary cases. In the case of political representation, on the descriptive account, the notion of active legislative government is not just theoretically obscure but can be perceived as a violation of the legislature's properly informational role. Yet the giving of information is presumed, in itself, to constitute an essential *critical* action. Thus again Mill, as quoted by Pitkin: "Instead of the function of governing, for which it is radically unfit, the proper office of a representative assembly is to watch and control the government: to throw the light of publicity on its acts."[9] In the case of literary representation, a similar notion emerges both in repudiations of explicit didacticism and in the assumption, apparently shared by de Sousa, that literary complexity counters the tyranny of simplistic "moral principle."

There is nothing especially surprising about these connections between political and literary ideology, connections no doubt easily traceable to closely related origins in eighteenth- and nineteenth-century liberal thought. What *is* surprising, perhaps, is the persistent endorsement of the critical force of literary complexity even in the work of writers ostensibly hostile either to liberalism or to its notion of rational moral progress (to both of which de Sousa is unembarrassedly loyal). Thus Derek Attridge, in the course of his energetic deconstructive updating of the idea of a distinctive literary language, quotes and endorses Paul de Man's claim, in his essay "The Resistance to Theory," that "the linguistics of literariness is a powerful and indispensable tool in the unmasking of ideological aberrations."[10] The reference to "linguistics" in this quotation is somewhat misleading, since de Manian readings typically focus on a text's linguistic features only insofar as such features (metaphors, puns, ambiguities, and so on) can be seen to occasion complex combinations and "re-castings" of what are really pre-existing "scenarios" in de Sousa's sense (that is, normative and quasi-conventional associations of objects and responses). To cite a now-classic instance, de Man's essay "The Purloined Ribbon" proceeds precisely by showing how a single crime confessed by Rousseau—the false accusation of a young maid-servant, Marion, to cover his own theft of a ribbon—can be seen as a bewilderingly elaborate complex scenario, in which the crime of cowardly slander is successively refigured (by devices too ingenious to summarize here) as an evasion of shame, an act of love, a gesture of self-display, and a sheer accident.[11]

In one respect, of course, de Man does intend the conflict of scenarios displayed by his reading to illustrate his deconstructive theory of language; as he himself puts it, "The main point of the reading [is] to show that the resulting predicament is linguistic rather than ontological or hermeneutic" ("PR," p. 45). What makes the predicament "linguistic" is the fact that the competing scenarios are brought together by means of a linguistic ambiguity (or at least what de Man takes to be such): when Rousseau said "Marion," he might have been performing any one of various speech acts, or no speech *act* at all (if "Marion" was an accident, just the first thing that popped into his head).[12] The undecidability of Rousseau's motives—the fact that his utterance is subject to a range of disparate explanations and therefore to a range of incompatible evaluations—is only symptomatic, for de Man, of the fundamental inappropriateness of every explanatory and evaluative scenario. To apply such a scenario to any utterance is to give referential content to what is really only a "fiction." It shows a "refusal to admit that fiction is fiction, [a] stubborn resistance to the fact, obvious by itself, that language is entirely free with regard to referential meaning and can posit whatever its grammar allows it to say" ("PR," p. 40).

I have elsewhere criticized the account of language that de Man develops in this essay.[13] My present interest, however, is not in de Man's doctrine of language as such but in its relation to his account of moral judgment, and therefore to his account, in "The Resistance to

Theory," of the ethical and political significance of "literariness." In one sense, the relation of literariness to moral judgment, on de Man's account, is entirely negative, since it defeats in advance every possible moral judgment:

> We know this to be the case from empirical experience as well: it is always possible to face up to any experience (to excuse any guilt), because the experience always exists simultaneously as fictional discourse and as empirical event and it is never possible to decide which one of the two possibilities is the right one. The indecision makes it possible to excuse the bleakest of crimes because, as a fiction, it escapes from the constraints of guilt and innocence.

But this way of neutralizing moral judgment is necessarily ineffective (no one *really* gets off the hook), for "it seems to be impossible to isolate the moment in which the fiction stands free of any signification; in the very moment at which it is posited, as well as in the context that it generates, it gets at once misinterpreted into a determination which is, *ipso facto,* overdetermined" ("PR," p. 40). In that sense, excuses, simply by presenting themselves as meaningful utterances, "generate the very guilt they exonerate, though always in excess or by default"; and indeed,

> No excuse can ever hope to catch up with such a proliferation of guilt. On the other hand, any guilt . . . can always be dismissed as the gratuitous product of a textual grammar or a radical fiction: there can never be enough guilt around to match the text-machine's power to excuse. Since guilt, in this description, is a cognitive and excuse a performative function of language, we are restating the disjunction of the performative from the cognitive: any speech act produces an excess of the cognitive, but it can never hope to know the process of its own production (the only thing worth knowing). ("PR," p. 45).

From one point of view, then, moral judgment is radically vitiated; but at the same time, this discovery is no good to any potential subject of moral blame. There is no way for an agent actually to evade moral judgment, since any speech act, even an assertion that moral judgment is inapplicable, generates a "cognitive" context that makes moral judgment (seem) applicable all over again.

Recently, discoveries about de Man's own past (his journalistic activities for a collaborationist newspaper in occupied Belgium) have raised the question of whether his account of guilt and excuses might have had an autobiographical referent.[14] But whatever its personal meaning may have been for de Man himself, his account of moral judgment stands in an odd relation to the claims for the ethical/political power of "literariness" advanced in "The Resistance to Theory." How can the "linguistics of literariness" constitute a "powerful and indispensable tool for unmasking ideological aberrations" if the lesson of "fiction" is that every speech act—including every act of "unmasking" aberrations—can be understood as such only insofar as it invites interpretation and therefore the aberrant imputation of meaning to what is really, on de Man's account, a "random" or "mechanical" event?[15] If anything, an attempt to unmask aberrations would seem to be doubly aberrant: it not only invites its own misinterpretation but perversely ascribes cognitive and moral content to the texts whose aberrations it claims to unmask.

In short, the attempt to found a literary critique of ideology on the radical freedom of "fiction" from cognitive and moral judgments is obviously self-defeating. For as de Man himself clearly indicates, his moral skepticism, based as it is on a skeptical account of interpretation in general, embraces not only moral judgments but, equally, all attempts to evade or criticize them. This outcome is so obvious, in fact, that it seems almost a programmatic feature of deconstructive claims to ethical and political relevance. Almost equally obvious is the degree to which, for all *practical* purposes, it reproduces the liberal predicament of "descriptive representation." Theoretically, of course, de Man's account is radically *anti*-representational ("Fiction has nothing to do with representation but is the absence of any link between utterance and a referent"; "PR," p. 39). For de Man, the space of the literary is constituted not by the tolerated conflict of competing scenarios but by the impossibility of legitimately applying *any* scenario to the "random errors" of language. Still, the outcome of his account of the literary matches the implicit outcome of de Sousa's: in both accounts, a power to criticize "aberrant" ideologies is imputed to structures of moral undecidability that actually turn out to be either hostile or indifferent to particular critical judgments.

The moral, so far, of this investigation of the relations between literary representation and morality would seem to be that the literary as such is devoid of moral significance. This seems to be the case even if one tries, like de Sousa, to construe moral values strictly

in terms of human emotive scenarios (and thus to eschew both Platonic moral realism and Kantian moral rationalism). For if one continues to believe, like de Sousa, in moral progress, then what should
matter is the substitution of good scenarios for bad ones (egalitarian
ones for racist ones), and it is hard to see how that aim is furthered
by inserting a given situation into a complex network of competing
scenarios. Even if complexity still permits an eventual subordination
of one (simple) scenario to another, the reason for choosing which
one to subordinate will have to come from somewhere outside the
complex scenario. Such a reason will necessarily seem arbitrary from
the perspective of the complex scenario itself—like an "interest
group" that usurps authority over a legislature that is supposed to
stand for everyone.

And that, of course, is precisely de Man's point: undecidability
makes preference arbitrary. For de Man, the literary is thus opposed (as
it were) "in principle" to rational progress. But the literary turns out
to lack even the negative significance that de Man ascribes to it. For
the attempt to convert undecidability itself into an instrument, if not
of moral progress then at least of resistance to ideology, depends on a
theory of necessary aberration that, if valid, neutralizes in advance the
particular critical judgments it promises.

Action and Reflection

I began this chapter by observing that literature, conceived as a range
of historically diverse institutions and practices, may well confer a
range of benefits on those who read and study its products. I could
have added that its harms may be equally numerous and important;
they are certainly as difficult to count or measure. The right conclusion
to draw, in my view, is that it makes no sense, on any axiological
theory, to assess the *general* costs and benefits of any very large and
various set of institutions and practices. And so far it seems equally
difficult to say anything very general about the benefits of literary
interest as such—which is to say, recalling the definition given earlier,
"an interest in representations that construct new compositions of
thought and value out of pre-existing relations between objects and
the responses associated with them." Whatever may be the specific
benefits of particular literary works in particular social contexts, the
right conclusion to draw about the ethical and political benefits of lit-

erary interest *in general and as such* seems to be, so far, that there may
not be any.

This conclusion is bound to seem counterintuitive to a fairly wide
range of readers and scholars, especially at a time when a new sense of
moral and political urgency has infused the rhetoric, at least, of academic literary debate. The sense of urgency no doubt derives from considerations that are extrinsic to the kind of formal interest peculiar to
literary criticism in its deconstructive as well as its New Critical and
(as I will later suggest) New Historicist versions. At present, it is
motivated by such questions as what constitutes a "culture"; whether
the selection of books to read should reflect or counteract the diversity
of available cultures; what role models are the right ones for young
readers; whether literary classrooms are or are not appropriate or, if
appropriate, useful sites of political organization. But these issues of
pedagogical policy, pressing as they are in the present academic context, seem hard to connect, in any direct or compelling way, to the
nature of literary representation as such. They can of course be linked
allegorically to literary structure; for instance, it is easy enough to alle-
gorize the composite structure of literary scenarios as an emblem either
of cultural diversity or of its putative conversion into a single national
identity. To do so, however, is merely to institute another version of
"descriptive representation"; for there is no non-arbitrary way to generate a practical movement, either toward or away from actual cultural
diversity, out of the mere formal possibility of mapping diversity
against complexity.

But even if the sense of urgency in present debates derives from
sources outside literary interest as such, the intuition that literary representation must have *some* kind of intrinsic relevance to our ethical
and political projects is hard to dispel. What accounts for it?

Consider what is likely to happen when a conventionally socialized
Western reader encounters a work like Chinua Achebe's novel *Things
Fall Apart*.[16] The novel begins by describing traditional Ibo society as
exemplified by a village in pre-colonial Nigeria, where life, though
rich in myth and ritual, is also dominated by harsh patriarchal customs, as well as by the arbitrary and sometimes murderous pronounce-
ments of mysterious oracles. Achebe then goes on to narrate the
alternately insidious and brutal process by which Ibo society is con-
quered by European Christianity and colonialism. To regret the
passing of the Ibo way of life is by implication to tolerate the extreme

subordination of women, the exposure of twins, and the murder, if the oracle so commands, of an adopted child; but to condemn these practices is, in the terms of the novel, to align oneself with the invading missionaries and colonialists.

Achebe's novel provides an impressively stark instance of a "complex scenario" in de Sousa's sense: the European intervention into traditional Ibo culture is presented simultaneously—though only, of course, for a reader who has previously learned the responses appropriate to each scenario—as a cruel act of aggression and as the only available answer to the often extreme injustices of Ibo custom. (Thus the first converts to Christianity are precisely the victimized and marginalized members of Ibo society, including effeminate men, women who have borne twins, *osu* or untouchable outcasts, and morally disaffected people like the protagonist's own son, unable to reconcile himself to the ritual murder of a hostage who had become, in effect, his adopted brother.)[17] Of course it is conceivable that a particular reader's predisposition in favor of one or the other of these scenarios will cause her simply to ignore the other; if that happens, however, the representation ceases to count, for that reader, as a complex scenario. And in that case, the reader's response to the novel ceases to differ in any important way from her response to any reported or imagined situation.

But suppose the reader does respond in the right way to both scenarios combined by Achebe's novel. Why is that a better thing to do than to respond to each scenario separately? Why, in other words, is reading the novel any better, morally speaking, than reading two *different* accounts, one of a just intervention on behalf of oppressed people and the other of a destructive colonial conquest? One answer might be that colonialism just *is* a morally ambiguous phenomenon, and that Achebe has accurately captured its true moral nature. But, for reasons that began to emerge in the discussion of de Sousa, that conclusion goes beyond anything contained within the novel's complex scenario itself. Nothing in the fact that a situation *can* be seen and responded to in various ways shows that it *should* be variously seen and responded to. Someone might easily argue that Achebe's portrait of Ibo society falsely mitigates the horror of colonial conquest by exaggerating pre-colonial injustices; or perhaps that the very complexity of Achebe's scenario falsely implies that feminism and anti-colonialism are incompatible.[18] Even if one thinks Achebe is right about colonialism, the novel's moral interest will derive from its having what one *already* has reason to think is the right account of colonialism. In other words, this will simply be a case in which literary complexity happens to match (what one takes to be) the complexity of a moral truth. But whether it really does so is undecidable on grounds internal to the literary representation itself.

There may be another way, however, to explain why a single complex scenario should seem to possess an unusual moral interest. A number of philosophers have recently denied that ethical claims are grounded either in an objective moral reality or in necessary conditions of practical reasoning; instead, these philosophers argue, the only plausible ground of ethical values is "people's dispositions."[19] Whether or not such an account of ethics is ultimately satisfactory, it seems hard to deny that a given person's ethical values are inseparable, if they are even distinguishable, from that person's dispositions to respond in certain ways to certain kinds of actions and situations. The issue contested among realist, rationalist, and "dispositionalist" philosophers can only be whether dispositions correspond to, or are otherwise grounded in, anything outside or deeper than themselves (such as human nature, divine commands, or the laws of rationality itself). If realists or rationalists are right, then our values can be wrong, whether or not we ever find this out; if dispositionalists are right, then our values derive from dispositions that can go wrong only by conflicting with other, stronger (or perhaps deeper) dispositions. But the issue can't be whether our values present themselves to us as *our* dispositions. For even a divine command will seem *ethically* binding only to someone who believes God issued it and is disposed to honor God's will, and even a law of rationality will seem binding only to someone who wants to be rational; indeed, no ethical consideration at all will seem binding to someone who doesn't want to be ethical.[20]

Perhaps, then, the moral benefit of literary interest lies not in any capacity to tell us which values are the right ones, but far more modestly, in the way it helps us find out what our evaluative dispositions *are*. Perhaps a complex scenario sets up a kind of experiment in which we test not the moral worth of one scenario against another one, as de Sousa suggests, but the relative strengths of our own responses to the alternative scenarios. By this means, one might discover, for instance, which of one's dispositions were out of line with the rest of one's motivational makeup. Reading Achebe's novel, a feminist anti-colonialist might discover that her negative response to patriarchal customs far outweighed her commitment to preserving indigenous cultures (or the reverse). And such a discovery might even lead to a certain attempt to change her dispositions in order to enhance their consistency—for instance by reducing the severity of her response to patriarchy, or by revising her stance toward Western interventions.

Suppose we grant, then, that encountering complex scenarios is likely to increase a reader's self-consciousness about her ethical and political dispositions, or at least about the relative *strengths* of various dispositions. (And in fact, I see no reason to doubt this.) The benefit of literary interest still remains ambiguous. For it still isn't clear exactly why we should value ethical and political self-consciousness. It still isn't clear, for instance, that the reader mentioned in the last paragraph is in any way better off—or politically more effective—once she discovers the inconsistency of her responses. Nothing in Achebe's novel can tell her *that,* any more than it can tell her which way to go if she decides to do something about the inconsistency. (And this is true even if one holds that dispositions are all there is to moral or any other kind of value.)

Why, then, should we value self-consciousness? Here the dispositionalist can give a simple and straightforward answer, one that is unavailable to the realist or the rationalist. The dispositionalist can say that we *should* value self-consciousness because we *do* value it. The kind of person we happen to value—by no means the kind of person valued at every time in every human society—is the kind that wants to check itself out, know how it feels, be aware of its inconsistencies, whether or not fixing them is either possible or desirable. Whether or not its particular choices and actions are the right ones from some external perspective, we might just say that such a person fits in better with our modern, Western, liberal, quasi-democratic form of life. (My account at this point experiments with the tone, and some of the spirit, of Richard Rorty.)[21]

But why, exactly, will such a person fit in so well with our form of life (our form, that is, if we are modern Western liberal quasi-democrats)? Part of the answer was already implicit in the remarks about liberal government in the previous section. A person who discovers, by reading literature, the conflicts, inconsistencies, and overdeterminations among her own dispositions is a person who can read *herself* as an instance of descriptive representation. She therefore encounters in herself an analogue of the predicament that Pitkin detected in a descriptively representative legislature: how to choose a particular course of action without suppressing the competing interests that all have a right to be registered in the same representational space. She finds herself embodying the ascendancy of information over action, of representation over authority, of "thick description" over simplifying principle,[22] that reappears at various levels of the liberal state.

This is not to say, however, that the governmental predicament described by Pitkin somehow *explains* the attractiveness of complex literary representations, or the value we seem to place on the style of self-consciousness they foster. The analogy between a liberal interest in literature and the predicament of liberal government points, I think, to a deeper connection between literary interest and the liberal conception of free agency as such. Here, it seems to me, the Lockean account of free agency is especially illuminating. Earlier conceptions of freedom tended to locate freedom either in the spontaneity of the will or in the free agent's direct apprehension of a substantive good. Rejecting these conceptions, Locke defines freedom solely in terms of the mind's capacity to suspend its decisions until it has had time to consider all its competing desires and their objects (at which point the suspension ceases—and so does freedom):

> For the mind having in most cases, as is evident in Experience, a power to *suspend* the execution and satisfaction of any of its desires, and so all, one after another, is at liberty to consider the objects of them; examine them on all sides, and weigh them with others . . . This seems to me the source of all liberty; in this seems to consist that, which is (as I think improperly) call'd *Free will.* For during this *suspension* of any desire, before the *will* be determined to action, and the action (which follows that determination) done, we have opportunity to examine, view, and judge, of the good or evil of what we are going to do.[23]

Clearly what Locke has in mind is something akin to the Davidsonian Principle of Continence that was borrowed and revised, as we saw, by de Sousa. To reflect before acting is to have a better chance of taking into account whatever reasons there are, instead of allowing one's actions to be ruled tyrannically by whatever passion first imposes itself. But this picture of freedom has an inherent difficulty not all that far removed from the predicament of government by descriptive representation: if freedom is conceived as involving reflection on the range of options (in place, once again, of a direct apprehension of the Good), then settling on any particular option can look more like a betrayal of freedom than its fulfillment. Conversely, the purest expression of freedom would seem to be a capacity to refrain from deciding at all; to remain "in uncertainties, Mysteries, doubts" and therefore in what already resembles the "impractical stasis" produced by literary interest.[24] And this suggests one last reason why an interest in complex literary representations can *feel* ethically or politically significant even if there is no plausible way to connect it to some particular ethical or political value. It isn't that literary interest makes someone a better agent. But it does give an unusually pure experience of what liberal agency, for better or worse, is like.[25]

And yet there is something unsatisfying about the historicism of the account I have just given. At the very least it seems somewhat hasty in its assumption that the apparent importance of self-consciousness to practical agency is merely a contingent feature of a certain moment in what is loosely called "Western history." It isn't yet clear that this assumption will survive a closer look at what practical agency may logically entail. That closer look will be taken in Chapter 5, after which it will be possible (in the Conclusion) to push the foregoing inquiry one step further.

Literary Interest outside Literature

In one important respect, my argument in this and the previous chapter has been potentially misleading. It has tended to focus (with the partial exception of the discussion of Paul de Man) on accounts of literary works as traditionally understood; more important, it has focused on accounts of texts, as if a complex scenario, in order to count as an object of the kind of interest I have been analyzing, had to be instantiated in a particular, pre-existing verbal artifact.

In recent years, however, the most obvious tendency of academic literary criticism—a tendency associated with, but by no means confined to, what has come to be called the New Historicism—has been to extend the scope of literary interest to include social and historical formations that can be seen as formally analogous to literary representations in the narrow sense.[26] Sometimes this tendency is justified by reference to theories, such as Foucault's, that seem to authorize the depiction of historical epochs or collective "discourses" as quasi-intentional agents.

But there is no need to personify historical and social formations in order to convert them into appropriate objects of literary interest, and it is crucial to see why. On the view I have defended in earlier chapters and in other writings, the object of literary *interpretation* is necessarily the meaning intended by some agent or collectivity of agents. But the object of literary *interest* is not an intended meaning; in fact, it isn't literally a *meaning* at all. The object of literary interest is a special kind of representational structure, each of whose elements acquires, by virtue of its connection with other elements, a network of associations inseparable from the representation itself. Thus, as we saw in the previous chapter, to be interested in regicide, as it appeared in *Macbeth,* was not to be interested in regicide as such but in regicide as set in its "galaxy of symbols"—regicide, that is, as suggesting, and suggested by, the thoughts and emotions appropriate to daggers, and crows, and naked babes, and so on.

But there is no reason why a structure eliciting an interest in the mutual implications of its elements can't be produced by accident, or by historical mechanisms transcending anyone's intentions. In this sense, a theorist like de Man can be wrong about literary language and still be right about the logic of literary overdetermination. And the New Critics, though wrong to think that literary interpretation could dispense with intention, were right in noticing that literary *interest* could do so. It isn't necessary, for the sake of literary interest, to settle on an intentional or non-intentional explanation—or *any* explanation—of how the relevant structure was produced. Thus the obvious explanatory vagueness of much New Historicist work—its failure to give any convincing reason for deciding, for instance, whether the theater in a particular era is an effect or a cause of a certain monarchical ideology, or whether a style of legal discourse causes or is caused by analogous features of contemporary medicine—is beside the point. For the point is to see how the theater, as it exists in its hard-to-define relation to the state, becomes (to someone who notices the right affinities) the theater as suggesting, and suggested by, the state.

But after all (returning to the question of value), why *bother* to extend the range of literary interest beyond the sphere of literary artifacts in the traditional sense? One powerful answer is that there is no reason not to. A second answer, perhaps equally powerful, is that shifting literary interest from literary artifacts to the social context in which those artifacts are produced or received can yield the *indirect and contingent* benefit of motivating an interest in important social phenomena that might otherwise be forgotten or ignored. A third, more intriguing but also more problematic answer is suggested by certain persistent emphases in the rhetoric of current critical debate. This third answer is that shifting critical attention from literary artifacts to their social and historical contexts is a way of giving literary interest the intrinsic and/or highly general ethical and political importance it otherwise lacks.

At first sight, this answer seems eminently plausible; indeed, it may even seem to remove the scandal of impractical absorption that lies, as we saw in the previous chapter, at the heart of the Platonic critique of poetry. If the scandal of literary interest consists in its fostering an irresponsible fixation on verbal artifacts, why not turn that fixation to socially responsible uses by making some a portion of social reality itself the object of fascination? Why wouldn't this make literary interest itself socially responsible (when employed in this way)? Or should we say that it gives rise to a new, quasi-literary mode of interest that necessarily *is* responsible, in virtue of its real-world objects?

The trouble with this suggestion, however, is that it overlooks what happens to one's interest in a social phenomenon (or anything else) once that phenomenon is reconfigured in such a way as to become an object of quasi-literary fascination. An interest in the-Tudor-state-as-suggestive-of-and-suggested-by-the-theater is no longer very clearly an interest in the state—the state, that is, as it might be found and analyzed in a range of contexts beyond the peculiarities of England under the Tudors. Once again, an interest in the former may indeed contingently foster an interest in the latter, and it may have a better chance of doing so under a New Historicist than under a New Critical regime. But it remains unclear how being absorbed in the cross-referential structure of an actual social phenomenon is, in itself, any more useful than being absorbed in a literary representation of the same phenomenon—unless, perhaps, one ought to feel a special kind of ethical gravity in the pull of the actual itself.

5

Collective Memory and
the Actual Past

Narrative and Normativity

Probably no one doubts that ethical and political dispositions depend on narratives.[1] Having a sense of what ought to be done is inseparable, if it is even distinguishable, from being committed to certain patterns of action—that is to say, to certain repeatable narrative forms. Possibly the most important narratives in this respect are simple ones, like the "paradigm scenarios" that have played a key role in the preceding two chapters. Such narratives, no doubt, are mostly learned in childhood and involve highly stereotypical situations, characters, and responses. But it seems clear that, subject to the qualifications developed in the previous chapter, even the narratives embedded in highly elaborate literary scenarios can sometimes play a role in shaping people's dispositions. And if dispositions sometimes depend on such complex narratives, then socially shared dispositions are likely to be connected with complex narratives preserved by collective memory, for example by oral tradition or a canonical literature. Beyond the *causal* role they play in influencing people's dispositions, the narratives preserved by collective memory sometimes play a *normative* role—that is, they may in various ways provide criteria, implicit or explicit, by which contemporary models of action can be shaped or corrected, or even by which particular ethical or political proposals can be authorized or criticized.[2] For convenience, I will speak of a narrative that possesses such normative status as bearing collective *authority*.

The question that concerns me, then, is this: why should it ever matter, if it does, that an authoritative narrative correspond to, or have anything much to do with, historical *actuality?* What, for instance, is the relation between a narrated act's paradigmatic authority and that act's actually having taken place at some specifiable moment, or *any* moment, in the past? The question sounds abstract, but in fact numerous concrete projects in various interpretive disciplines seem to involve, or at least to suggest, the claim that historical actuality matters; that, for instance, the political role played in the present by a canonical text ought to be reformed in such a way as to connect it to an unmasked or demystified account of the actual historical conditions under which the text was produced. Sometimes this claim finds expression in an attempt to use the exposure of social origins as a means of emptying a canonical text of its traditional prestige; in other cases, the point is not simply to reject the canonical narrative but to transfer its authority, once its historical falsity has been exposed, to politically desirable features of the actual past that the text has either distorted or suppressed. Either way, an assumption implicit in a number of current critical tendencies, including a range of feminist, Marxist, and New Historicist treatments of canonical texts, seems to be that foregrounding the actual circumstances from which a certain work emerged has a necessary or intrinsic relevance to ethical and political action in the present. At least it is hard to see why, unless the benefits are assumed to be necessary or intrinsic, critics who insist on the political urgency of reconstructing social origins so seldom mention what *contingent* or *extrinsic* benefits the reconstructions are supposed to have.

In the previous chapter, I presented an essentially skeptical (though still provisional) account of the notion that an interest in the complex structures of literary representation was intrinsically of ethical or political benefit. In one sense, the assumption I have just described may signal a desire to ground the relevance of literary interest not in an alleged critical power of literary form itself but, on the contrary, in a demystifying turn away from a classic literary representation and toward the social reality from which it emerged. One way to make sense of this desire is to suppose that the recovery of past social reality is itself somehow ethically or politically valuable. My aim in what follows will be to explore the grounds and implications of this supposition, at first by examining the role it plays in three recent proposals, two from the field of biblical criticism and one from the criticism of secular canonical literature. While my treatment of these proposals will be critical, my purpose in considering them is not primarily polemical; I will be using these examples mainly to suggest the difficulty of accounting, in any very simple or straightforward way, for an investment in the actual collective past as such.

Historical Reconstruction and Scriptural Authority

The practice of turning from internal commentary on the Bible to a reconstruction of its origins is not, of course, a recent development; for more than two centuries, historically minded scholars have attempted to recover the lost referents of the biblical texts by reconstructing the stages of oral and written composition supposed to lie behind the texts as we have them. Mainstream theology since the Enlightenment has been characterized by a succession of attempts either to neutralize the corrosive force of such criticism or, more remarkably, to turn alleged discoveries of the Bible's historical inaccuracies to positive theological and apologetic uses.[3] One prominent strategy earlier in this century, associated with such terms as "neo-orthodoxy," "dialectical theology," and "biblical theology," was to concede the historical contingency of the Bible's origins, only to insist with renewed vigor on the universal authority of its theological content (or at least its existential resonance). Since the collapse two decades ago of what had seemed to many observers a neo-orthodox consensus, theological initiative has passed to political theologies that seem on the whole indifferent to the specific findings of historical criticism. Indeed, Third World and feminist liberation theologians are often reproached, even by sympathetic critics, for making highly selective and uncritical use of the Bible—emphasizing politically attractive episodes, such as the Exodus or the Magnificat ("he has put down the mighty from their thrones, and exalted those of low degree; he has filled the hungry with good things, and the rich he has sent empty away"), without considering their historical referents or their precise ideological functions.

Recently biblical criticism has seen the rise of a tendency whose explicit aim is to bridge the gap between critical scholarship and political theology. Behind this tendency is a belief that two obstacles currently stand in the way of liberationist attempts to appropriate historical criticism: first, the elitist and androcentric biases of the major historical-critical scholars; second, the ideological distortions of social and political realities introduced into the Bible by the biblical writers or redactors themselves. The only way to correct for such distortions, according to proponents of the current tendency, is through the rigorous application of social-historical and other "materialist" methods. Hence the call for a shift of critical efforts away from analyses of the biblical text and toward a reconstruction of the social conditions presumed to lie behind it.

My aim in this section will not be to endorse or criticize the methods scholars are using to reconstruct the Bible's social origins; I am neither a biblical scholar nor a social historian. Nor am I concerned here with the broader epistemological question of whether and in what sense historical research can ever hope to reconstruct the "actual" past. My interest is in the reconstructive impulse itself, or more precisely, in the impulse to go behind the official memories recorded in canonical texts, religious or otherwise, to get at the social facts those "memories" have allegedly suppressed or forgotten. The current sociological or materialist tendency in biblical criticism constitutes an especially telling instance of this impulse, not simply because it is reconstructive (old-fashioned historical criticism already was that) but because the explicit turn from text to social reality makes the break with traditional memory unusually stark. After all, their focus on literary or quasi-literary stages of composition (for instance, the oral traditions supposed to have preceded the successive states of the text) enabled the older historical critics to think of themselves as elaborating, rather then correcting, the memory preserved in the canonical texts. They could treat the texts as memory traces that were at least metonymically continuous with the compositional stages criticism reconstructed. Hence the great critical scholar and biblical theologian Gerhard von Rad could still view the writing down of an oral tradition not as abrogating but as preserving a story's relation to its specific historical function: "When the material was written down, it became fixed at a phase of its development in which a certain religious transformation had already occurred, but when, notwithstanding, the historical element was preserved undissipated and with the full import of uniqueness."[4] But sociological reconstruction—at least as practiced in the salient examples I will consider—involves a conception of the canonical texts not as partial memories but as forms of more or less willful amnesia. My examples, the titles of which alone would make them irresistibly apt for my purposes, are Norman K. Gottwald's massive study *The Tribes of Yahweh: A Sociology of the Religion of Liberated Israel, 1250–1050 B.C.E.* and Elisabeth Schüssler Fiorenza's *In Memory of Her: A Feminist Theological Reconstruction of Christian Origins.*[5]

Gottwald's subject is the surprising emergence of Israelite society as an independent "intertribal confederacy" in an environment dominated by oppressive city-states. His main historical thesis is not itself original but consists in his endorsement of the so-called "revolt model," a hypothetical explanation of Israel's origins that was introduced by George E. Mendenhall in 1962.[6] In contrast to the views that Israel was established in Canaan either by gradual immigration or by the direct military conquest narrated in the Book of Joshua, the revolt model suggests that Israel first arose as a coalition of oppressed and disaffected people within or on the margins of the Canaanite city-states. Premonarchic Israel is thus, according to Gottwald, "most appropriately conceived as an eclectic composite in which various underclass and outlaw elements of society joined their diffused antifeudal experiences, sentiments, and interests, thereby forming a single movement that, through trial and error, became an effective autonomous social system" (*TY,* p. 491). Once again, the model is not itself original; what is original, apart from the methodological tenacity with which Gottwald pursues Mendenhall's hypothesis, is Gottwald's transformation of the revolt model into a total explanation of Israel's distinctive theology. According to Gottwald, Israel's theological uniqueness is an expression of its singularity as an egalitarian, "retribalized" society, established through constant revolutionary opposition to the hierarchical structures and interests from which it emerged and which constantly threatened to reabsorb it. The religion of Yahweh, though not a mere reflection of this egalitarian social order, is best conceived as a "symbolic projection" or "ideological formation" designed to promote egalitarian social relations. The salvation narrative that formed the core of Yahwism functioned, to use Gottwald's metaphors, as a kind of "feedback loop" or "servomechanism," reinforcing and regulating the social practices by which it was produced (*TY,* pp. 646–647). Consequently—and it is here that the scope of Gottwald's revisionism becomes fully visible—all the major distinctive features of

Israelite theology can and must be translated into social terms. "In brief," Gottwald writes,

> the chief articles of Yahwistic faith may be socioeconomically "demythologized" as follows: "Yahweh" is the historically concretized, primordial power to establish and sustain social equality in the face of counter-opposition from without and against provincial and nonegalitarian tendencies from within the society. "The Chosen People" is the distinctive self-consciousness of a society of equals created in the intertribal order and demarcated from a primarily centralized and stratified surrounding world. "Covenant" is the bonding of decentralized social groups in a larger society of equals committed to cooperation without authoritarian leadership and a way of symbolizing the locus of sovereignty in such a society of equals. "Eschatology," or hope for the future, is the sustained commitment of fellow tribesmen to a society of equals with the confidence and determination that this way of life can prevail against great environmental odds. (*TY,* p. 692)

Gottwald's reconstruction applies not only to theological concepts but to the narratives in which those concepts are embedded: the early biblical narrative paradigms, such as "Deliverance from Egypt" and "Conquest of the Land," all possess, in his view, a single "proper and immediate referent . . . : contemporary liberated and retribalized Israel in Canaan." If this referent has fallen out of the collective memory of the numerous societies in which these narratives continue to exercise ethical and political authority, this is because it was largely suppressed during the monarchic period (beginning in the late eleventh century B.C.E.), when "liberation and retribalization was [*sic*] frustrated and in major respects cut short by the social evolution of Israel into a centralized state with internal social stratification," although the premonarchic tendencies to some extent persisted, for instance in the prophetic movement (*TY,* p. 698). Schüssler Fiorenza's aims and findings are in striking ways similar to Gottwald's; her book has the added advantage here of making an explicit connection between politically motivated historical reconstruction and the notions of collective memory and amnesia. Her historical thesis is that Christianity originated in a sequence of two social movements: an egalitarian "Jesus movement" within first-century Palestinian Judaism and a movement of Christians properly so called, which emerged in the decades following Jesus' death and spread rapidly to Hellenized Jewish communities throughout the Mediterranean region. Unfortunately, according to Schüssler Fiorenza, our primary access to the social reality of these movements is through apologetic documents whose ideological function was precisely to domesticate the radical thrust of early Christianity—above all, to neutralize the threat Christian egalitarianism posed to the patriarchal structures of Mediterranean societies, Jewish and Gentile alike. In Schüssler Fiorenza's view, the New Testament documents display a pervasive and systematic tendency to suppress the evidence of egalitarianism particularly in regard to women, whose crucial leadership roles were all but erased from the Church's official memory.

In some cases the evidence of distortion is obvious. Paul's letters, for instance, frequently mention women as co-workers, with the same role and authority as Paul himself (*MH,* p. 169). But in the later-written Lucan history of the missionary movement, the so-called "Acts of the Apostles," leadership is concentrated in the figure of Paul and several male colleagues, while women are restricted to the roles of either "auxiliary supporters or influential opponents of Paul's mission" (*MH,* p. 161). In other cases, correcting for the androcentric bias of the New Testament writers and redactors means using the full panoply of historical-critical strategies, though these strategies need to be supplemented by "methodological rules for a feminist hermeneutics of suspicion" (*MH,* p. 108). But in every case, the direction of Schüssler Fiorenza's revisionism is clear: it "seeks to move," as she succinctly puts it, "from androcentric texts to patriarchal-historical contexts" (*MH,* p. 29).

Perhaps the most compelling example of Schüssler Fiorenza's approach is her treatment of the Gospel episode that suggested her title, *In Memory of Her.* All four Gospels include the story of a woman who anoints Jesus with a costly ointment. In two Gospels (Mark and Matthew) the woman anoints Jesus' head; in the other two (Luke and John) she anoints his feet. Schüssler Fiorenza argues that the first of these versions of the anointing is the earlier one, and she reconstructs the story's original point accordingly: "Since the prophet in the Old Testament anointed the head of the Jewish king, the anointing of Jesus' head must have been understood immediately as the prophetic recognition of Jesus, the Anointed, the Messiah, the Christ. According to the tradition it was a woman who named Jesus by and through her prophetic sign-action." But this, Schüssler Fiorenza notes, "was a politically dangerous story" (*MH*, p. xiv). Its original point was consequently suppressed by the Gospel redactors, who sought, she reasons, "to make the story more palatable to a patriarchal Greco-Roman audience" (*MH*, p. xiii). By the time the story appears in Luke—in its most famous and dramatic version—the woman has been changed from a prophetic disciple into a sinner, "a woman of the city," who wets Jesus' feet with her tears and wipes them with her hair (Luke 7:36–50). In Mark, the version Schüssler Fiorenza considers closest to the original, the unnamed woman is one of three disciples who play important roles in the passion narrative. The other two are Judas, the betrayer, and Peter, the denier of Jesus. When the woman anoints him, Jesus promises that "wherever the gospel is preached in the whole world, what she has done will be told in memory of her" (Mark 14:9). To which Schüssler Fiorenza pointedly responds: "Wherever the gospel is proclaimed and the eucharist celebrated another story is told: the story of the apostle who betrayed Jesus. The name of the betrayer is remembered, but the name of the faithful disciple is forgotten because she was a woman" (*MH*, p. xiii).

What consequences do such reconstructions have for the authority of biblical narratives? It is obvious that scriptural authority, for Gottwald and for Schüssler Fiorenza, shifts from the texts themselves to the historical events (mainly complex and inconclusive social struggles) of which the texts are, once again, severely distorted reflections.[7] Schüssler Fiorenza is especially insistent on the need to abandon all attempts to make the texts themselves a source of liberating authority. Her opening chapter sharply criticizes the "neo-orthodox model of feminist interpretation," that is, the attempt to isolate a special "canon within the canon," such as a set of liberationist principles expressed by so-called "prophetic" themes and patterns (*MH*, pp. 14–21). In contrast to this approach, her own model refuses to "identify revelation with the androcentric text, but maintains that such revelation is found in the life and ministry of Jesus as well as in the discipleship community called forth by him" (*MH*, p. 34).

What may seem surprising in such proposals is the way revisionists like Gottwald and Schüssler Fiorenza, in relocating the Bible's authority, stop short of simply rejecting it. On the face of it this move may seem logically odd; for what sense does it make to cling to a tradition, the handing down of an ancient authority, when the grounds and content of that authority have been so drastically reconceived? I will return to this problem in a later section; for now I wish to concentrate on a somewhat different implication of the proposal to shift the locus of scriptural authority from an officially remembered to a reconstructed narrative. The intriguing question raised by Gottwald's and Schüssler Fiorenza's reconstructions is not whether it makes sense to revise a traditional faith but why social events in the distant past should matter to us at all—let alone claim the authority of scripture. It is one thing, after all, to grant authority to a text that one supposes was written, directly or indirectly, by God; on the assumption that God's mind hasn't changed since the text was written, one reads the text to find out what God (presently) wants. But the same thing cannot be said about historical events—unless one supposes that God providentially manipulated the events to produce a kind of dramatic or moving-pictorial writing. Doubtless this notion has traditional warrants, but it obviously collapses the distinction between text and event so completely that turning from one to the other, as the revisionists recommend, would be no different, fundamentally, from shifting one's attention from one passage to another, as interpreters have always done. In any case, reading social events as divinely inspired hieroglyphs can hardly be what Gottwald and Schüssler Fiorenza have in mind. A major point of social-historical reconstruction is presumably to demystify the notion that God intervenes in history in anything like the manner suggested by the image of divine pictography. Gottwald in particular is expressly hostile to that sort of supernaturalism; in an essay reflecting on his work in *The Tribes of Yahweh,* he writes of having "carried through a radical socioeconomic and religiocultural deconstruction of early Israel without leaving any remainder to save traditional theology by means of the ever-convenient 'god who fills the gaps.' "[8]

Where then, if not in their status as signs of (unaltered) divine intentions, does materialist criticism locate the scriptural authority of ancient events? The answer seems to lie in a peculiar combination of two kinds of relation between the present and the past: a combination of, on one hand, the relation of *analogy* and, on the other hand, sheer historical continuity. Specifically, the present authority of Israel's or of the Church's actual social origins is presumed to derive from the intersection of two relations: first, the perceived analogy between ancient and modern social struggles; second, the influence, however remote, that the ancient struggles have exerted on the struggles in which participants in the tradition are, or should be, presently engaged.

The principles of analogy and continuity, while not explicitly named by Schüssler Fiorenza, are implicitly combined in her insistence on the essential role of feminist memory. Biblical contexts are relevant to present feminist struggles because they provide the "roots and beginnings" of the "continuous history" of what Schüssler Fiorenza calls "women as the *ekklēsia* of God" (*MH*, p. 350). But ancient struggles are not merely early steps in a historical sequence that eventuates in modern feminism. Those struggles are also *similar* to present ones, so that remembering them "not only keeps alive the suffering and hopes of Christian women in the past but also allows for a universal solidarity of sisterhood with all women of the past, present, and future who follow the same vision" (*MH*, p. 31). The crucial point, once again, is the coincidence of continuity, which connects past and present via historical sequence, and analogy, which connects past and present via a property common to both—namely, the "vision" shared by ancient and modern feminists.[9]

Gottwald seems somewhat less confident than Schüssler Fiorenza that ancient and modern participants in the biblical tradition share "the same vision." The version of sociology Gottwald favors assumes that ideological products like "visions" are closely bound to the contexts from which they emerge. Hence, according to Gottwald, "To purport to believe the same things in different social and intellectual conditions is in fact not to believe the same things at all" (*TY*, p. 704). In general Gottwald seems less ready than Schüssler Fiorenza to suppose that we really can "continue to derive symbolic resources from the biblical traditions" (*TY*, p. 705). But *if* this is possible, then the basis of the possibility turns out once again to be a coincidence of analogy and continuity. Thus Israel's "powerful, evocative symbolism" helped it, Gottwald writes, to strive "for liberated life of a sort realizable under the socioeconomic and intellectual-cultural conditions peculiar to its time and place." Nevertheless, "*similar* struggles in great variety have punctuated the long history that *connects* us with early Israel" (*TY*, p. 705; emphasis added).

Similarity and connection, or again in my terms, analogy and continuity. Everything seems to hinge on the possibility of making these two relations coincide; neither one by itself seems sufficient to justify a sense that the truth about ancient struggles is intrinsically relevant to present ones. If an event in the past merely *resembles* one in the present, it may indeed provide us with "symbolic resources"—ways of representing our present values and intentions so as to shape and motivate our present actions. But in that case our sense of what is symbolically useful in the past will depend on our present sense of what matters, and the values represented by what we borrow from the past will only be the ones we already have. Aspects of the past that fail to match up with our present dispositions will necessarily seem irrelevant. When it comes to analogy, in other words, the lines of authority run from present to past and not the other way around.

Another way to get at this point is to ask whether it matters, except for convenience, that the narrated events providing the symbolic resources should actually have occurred in our own collective past—or indeed, that they should ever have occurred at all. If the value of the analogy lies in the fact that some other situation provides opportunities for representing our own judgments and desires, why not turn to other people's histories—or to fiction—for symbolic narratives as good as or better than the ones our own tradition happens to provide? Why aren't narratives of events in our actual past simply replaceable by other narratives that meet our criteria of symbolic relevance?

There is one obvious reason, however, why other people's pasts—and fictional narratives—may strike us as less useful than our own histories: they are incapable of satisfying our curiosity about our own origins; they fail to provide *explanations* of how we got where we are. When it comes to explanation, in contrast to analogy, the lines of force that matter are indeed those that run from past to present, and that do so following a particular and irreplaceable causal chain. But why should the fact that a past event has explanatory relevance to the present endow it with ethical or political authority in relation to present agents—unless, once again, it happens to correspond to the values those agents already have? The historian Edmund S. Morgan argues convincingly, for instance, that American ideals of freedom and equality can be traced in part to an ideology that arose in colonial Virginia, where the possession of even a few slaves gave a modicum of independence and social prestige to small landowners; "equality" thus meant solidarity among slaveholders.[10] If Morgan's explanation is correct, it is hard to see how such causal "roots and beginnings" of egalitarian values collectively affirmed in the present can function usefully as a means of symbolically promoting or reinforcing those values. Certainly the explanatory significance of the social reality Morgan reconstructs does not confer any present authority on that past reality; it's not as if one feels inclined, after reading Morgan's account, to advocate slaveholding as a way living up to one's egalitarian commitments. (I will return to Morgan—and to the question of what kinds of relevance the actual past may have even if it lacks intrinsic authority—in the last two sections.)

As this example suggests, the locus of authority is always in the present; we use, for promoting and reinforcing ethical and political dispositions, only those elements of the past that correspond to our sense of what presently compels us. In fact, not even a belief in the divine manipulation of history or the inspired inerrancy of scripture would really shift the locus of authority from the present to the past. Conservative believers simply assume that the power that expressed itself in divinely inspired texts or events is the same power that presently reigns over them—and that this power has not, in the meantime, changed its mind. Even for conservative believers, it is the supposed permanence of God's intentions—not a source of authority located in the actual past as such—that keeps the past alive and gives it a derived authority over the present.

If these points by now seem obvious, it is crucial to recognize how persistently they are obscured in current attempts to give revisionist interpretation an intrinsic ethical and political significance. The programmatic remarks I have excerpted from the writings of Gottwald and Schüssler Fiorenza exemplify what I take to be a primary logical mechanism by which a wide range of such attempts are sustained. For if the past is merely a source of analogies, particular past events may provide models for present action but are in principle expendable; they can all be replaced by analogies borrowed from other traditions or from fiction. If the past is merely a source of explanations, it may well be irreplaceable (there is no other way to explain how we got where we are), but ancestral actions of the greatest explanatory interest may express values remote from any we can now embrace. Hence the pressure to focus on historical phenomena whose *combination* of symbolic resonance and explanatory uniqueness will make these two benefits seem mutually dependent. But the fact that some events can function both as sources of authoritative images and as explanations of a present situation does not mean that seeking explanations and seeking authoritative images amount to the same operation; it does not mean, in other words, that a special ethical importance attaches to the actual as distinct from the remembered or the imagined past.

In the next section I will turn from the criticism of particular revisionist programs to a conceptual analysis of (some features of) our relation to the actual past. But first it is worth pausing to notice that the impulse to bridge the logical gap between analogy and explanation is not confined to biblical studies. In *The Political Unconscious,* Fredric Jameson attacks what he considers the twin forms of decadence in current literary criticism: the mere "antiquarianism" of traditional literary history and its "dialectical counterpart," which is, Jameson writes, "ultimately no more satisfactory: I mean the tendency of much contemporary theory to rewrite selected texts from the past in terms of its own aesthetic and, in particular, in terms of a modernist (or more properly post-modernist) conception of language."[11] In the terms used above, what Jameson dislikes is the division of critical attention between continuity and analogy, between the mere reconstruction of historical sequences and the use of past texts to stand for present values. The domination of literary studies by these two opposing tendencies presents, for Jameson, an "unacceptable option, or ideological double bind, between antiquarianism and modernizing 'relevance' or projection." But this dilemma only testifies to the lack of a "genuine philosophy of history" that will be "capable of respecting the specificity and radical difference of the social and cultural past while disclosing the solidarity of its polemics and passions, its forms, structures, experiences, and struggles with those of the present day" (*PU,* p. 18). In the past such a philosophy was provided by Christian typological thinking; Jameson's candidate for a modern replacement for Christian hermeneutics is Marxism. Only through Marxism, he writes,

> can we glimpse the vital claims upon us of such long-dead issues as the seasonal alternation of the economy of a primitive tribe, the passionate disputes about the nature of the Trinity, the conflicting models of the *polis* or the universal Empire, or, apparently closer to us in time, the dusty parliamentary and journalistic polemics of the nineteenth-century nation states. These matters can recover their original urgency for us only if they are retold within the unity of a single great collective story; only if, in however disguised and symbolic a form, they are seen as sharing a single fundamental theme—for Marxism, the collective struggle to wrest a realm of Freedom from a realm of Necessity; only if they are grasped as vital episodes in a single vast unfinished plot. (*PU,* pp. 19–20)

The wish behind this extraordinary scenario is not only related but I suggest identical to the wish that motivates Gottwald and Schüssler Fiorenza, and Jameson's program succumbs to the same dilemma. If anything the dilemma is heightened by his rigorous insistence on reading canonical literary works as products of the dominant ideologies in each period he analyzes. If the "single great collective story" Jameson envisions is not in fact a divinely constructed narrative but merely a causally related sequence of disparate ideologies, then its relevance to the present can only be established by one or another version of the modernizing "projection" Jameson attacks. Otherwise it remains unclear just what sort of value a modern reader is supposed to derive from a work produced under radically different conditions and in the service of someone else's ideology.

In his Conclusion, Jameson takes up precisely this question, which he recognizes his book has so far left unanswered: "How is it possible for a cultural text which fulfills a demonstrably ideological function . . . to resonate a universal value inconsistent with the narrower limits of class privilege which inform its more immediate ideological vocation?" (*PU*, p. 288). His surprising answer is that the expression of *any* class interest whatsoever, by the sheer fact that it expresses a collective solidarity, however vile or destructive, can be said to stand for a classless Utopia. In this sense, according to Jameson, "*all* class consciousness—or in other words, all ideology in the strongest sense, including the most exclusive forms of ruling-class consciousness just as much as that of oppositional or oppressed classes—is in its very nature Utopian" (*PU*, p. 289). Jameson's elaboration of this formula makes unmistakable its proximity to the kind of "projection" he earlier rejected:

> All class consciousness of whatever type is Utopian insofar as it expresses the unity of a collectivity; yet it must be added that this proposition is an allegorical one. The achieved collectivity or organic group of whatever kind—oppressors fully as much as oppressed—is Utopian not in itself, but only insofar as all such collectivities are themselves *figures* for the ultimate concrete life of an achieved Utopian or classless society. Now we are in a better position to understand how even hegemonic or ruling-class culture and ideology are Utopian, not in spite of their instrumental function to secure and perpetuate class privilege and power, but rather precisely because that function is also in and of itself the affirmation of collective solidarity. (*PU*, pp. 290–291)

To say that all literary works can be read as embodying the same vision, the same universal value, simply because they are all equally the products of collective interests, is to say that they can be read analogically: they can all be used as symbols of present Marxist values, provided only that we focus on the point of resemblance (namely, some affirmation of solidarity) and ignore everything that gives them their specific historical identity. Once again, explanatory interest and ethical or political value come apart. Jameson's program oscillates between explanation and analogy or, in his own harsher terms, antiquarianism and projection, and thus remains fixed in the "double bind" he deplores.

Collective Punishment

So far my argument has shown the error involved in a certain way of construing the present relevance of events in the collective past—the error, that is, of treating the coincidence of analogy and continuity as if it were an *identity* of those relations. The mere fact that something in the past can stand in a relation both of resemblance and of historical antecedence to present values is not enough to give it an intrinsic ethical or political importance. But surely the widespread intuition that the actual collective past is intrinsically relevant to present action cannot be reduced to the abstract terms in which the issue has been formulated so far. After all, even outside the sphere of academic criticism one encounters the demand that people be held accountable for their pasts, as well as the expectation that they will properly experience guilt, pride, regret, or a sense of obligation as a result of certain actions they once performed. Given the ubiquity of our practices of connecting people— and connecting ourselves—to what we think actually occurred the past, what can it mean to *deny* that the past has ethical claims on the present? And if it ever makes sense to insist on the inescapability of an agent's relation to that agent's personal past, does it make equal sense to bind an agent to the past of the collectivities in which he participates?[12] What, in short, is the difference between a personal and a collective past, and why isn't the latter at least as relevant to present action as the former?[13] The following reflections are not intended as an elaboration of the polemic in the previous section but as a new and largely independent attempt to address these questions.

Consider, then, a social practice that, perhaps more obviously than any other, assumes that past events have an intrinsic relevance to present action: the practice of punishment. By selecting this example, I do not mean to suggest that revisionist interpreters are committed to the value of collective punishment, though some of them may be. Nor do I wish to attack or defend the notion of punishment as such, let alone any specific use of punishment, collective or otherwise. In one crucial respect, to which I will return at the end of this section, the example of punishment may be positively misleading. Nevertheless, some of punishment's peculiar logical features may enable us to isolate the sources of the broader intuition that the past has an irreducible ethical claim on the present.[14] I assume throughout that the results of this analysis would, with adjustments, be applicable to other, less dramatic ways of connecting people to the actual past, such as rewarding them for past deeds performed by them or their ancestors, or holding them to personal or collective promises.

Reference to the actual past seems built into the notion of punishment from the start. (At least this is the case where punishment is intended to count as a just or ethically appropriate response to a reprehensible action. Where punishment is practiced without regard to justice and simply as a means of inducing obedience, actual guilt—and consequently any connection to actual past events—is plainly irrelevant.)[15] If the (ethical) point of punishing someone were not in some sense to repay the actual agent for some actual past act but merely to discourage people in general from performing certain actions in the future, it would not seem to matter whether the punishment itself was actual. Actual war criminals, for instance, could be replaced by actors who would then pay ingeniously faked penalties, being replaced, perhaps, on the scaffold or in their cells by mannequins. But someone who found out that the actual criminals were still living happily somewhere would no doubt feel unsatisfied.[16] The question is, would this feeling of dissatisfaction be justified if it turned out that ethically motivated punishment could have no other object but deterrence? If the aim of punishment is only to influence present and future behavior, why should we care about anyone's actual *past* behavior, given that it is obviously too late to deter an act that someone has already performed?

Apparently, then, punishment involves more than merely influencing present and future behavior; we seem to want to make certain that the actual agents are somehow affected by their past crimes. What would bother us, if we discovered that the war criminals had been replaced by actors, would be a vision of the actual criminals living happily after committing their heinous crimes. The point of our desire to punish them, on this account, is that punishing them is the only way to guarantee that they will experience the badness of their bad actions. Punishment of the actual agent makes sense on this account precisely because it is not a futile attempt to alter the past but is meant to produce a change in the agent *as he now exists;* he now experiences pleasure or insufficient pain in relation to his bad action, and we want that experience replaced by something more appropriate.

Unfortunately, however, the apparent discovery that what matters is the present state of the agent only raises a further question. For if what matters is the present state of the agent—if having an interest in the agent as he now exists is the only way to make sense of doing something to him *now*—then why should it matter that the action in question is one he actually performed? Why shouldn't we be equally ready to punish someone who takes pleasure in a crime he mistakenly believes (mistakenly "remembers") he committed? Or someone who takes pleasure in someone *else's* bad action? Why isn't taking pleasure in bad action sufficient by itself to warrant punishment? And why stop even there? Why not say that taking pleasure in anything bad—for instance, natural disasters—is equally deserving of punishment? Why should the past occurrence or non-occurrence of the act matter at all if what one is really interested in is producing desirable changes in the present state of the person in question?

Consider the defense of retributive punishment in Robert Nozick's *Philosophical Explanations.* According to Nozick, "An act of retribution is responsive to a wrong act as wrong. It effects a connection of the wrongdoer with correct values by being fully responsive to his wrong act in its character as a wrong act." Mere rehabilitation would be inadequate:

> To leave great wrongdoing unresponded to as wrong, substituting instead a beneficial transformation of the wrongdoer unrelated to the wrong in its content, is to ignore and be blind (in one's actions) to this significant portion of moral reality. At stake in addition to the punisher's response to wrongness as wrongness is the wrongdoer's response. Punishment links the wrongdoer with correct values, and is a vehicle whereby the nature and magnitude of his act's wrongness has a correspondingly significant effect in his life.[17]

Nozick stops short of asking, however, why the magnitude of the act's wrongness should have its effect specifically on the life of the wrongdoer. Why shouldn't it have an equally significant effect on the lives of all who *approve* the wrongdoer's act, if all that matters is that wrongness be appropriately responded to? The wrongdoer is not, after all, *now* actively "flouting" correct values in Nozick's sense; the fact that he *now* takes pleasure in the bad act, if in fact he does, in no way distinguishes him from anyone else who shares his reprehensible attitude. Why, then, should he be singled out for punishment?

Nozick's account seems to require a peculiarly strong notion of personal identity.[18] To make sense of Nozick's theory, one has to conceive the act itself—its actual performance and not just its *having occurred*—as a persistent feature of the agent's identity; only in that case would the agent's present relation to his past act differ (in kind or degree of wrongness) from that of someone who did not perform the act but merely shared his attitude toward it. But this would mean thinking of the agent as presently—if not eternally—performing the act he once performed; in what other way could the performing of the act (and not simply its having been performed) remain a continuously significant feature of the agent's identity?

The question, then, is whether it makes sense to treat a person existing in the present as still the appropriate object of attitudes appropriate to an action she performed in the past. Taken seriously, this can only mean thinking of her as still performing the act in question. For unless she is thought of as still performing the act, she may be in many respects the same person as the person who performed it, but she is in at least one crucial respect not identical to that person (as she *then* existed), since she no longer has any control over the act's occurring or not occurring; *she* has no more power over it than anyone else. Nor does it matter, in this connection, whether having such power is conceived in libertarian terms or determinist ones.[19] My point is not that she could not *then* have "done otherwise" than she did; my point is rather that her present relation to the act's occurring or not occurring is difficult to distinguish from anyone else's relation to it.[20] What originally set the agent apart from everyone else was her being in the moment of the act its actual performer. But the person who now exists, even if she remains uniquely identical to the person who performed the act, has lost her unique relation to the act itself—unless, once again, she can be thought of as somehow bound to the act in the way she would be if she were still performing it.[21]

Now it seems clear that people do think of themselves in precisely this way—for instance, they do so whenever they feel guilt or shame (or pride or satisfaction) in relation to some act they once performed. In fact, the foregoing analysis can be turned around in such a way as to show an inseparable link between thinking of oneself as essentially bound to one's own actual past and being able to distinguish oneself, in *any* significant way, from other agents who share the same attitudes and the same possibilities of future action. Insofar as my *possible* acts are concerned, I conceive myself, strictly speaking, not as a particular person but as exemplifying a *type* of person, someone who can be replaced by anyone who happens to share the same attitudes, abilities, and opportunities. My relation to possible acts I might perform, in other words, lacks the indexical particularity of my relation to whatever acts I actually did perform in my (utterly singular) past. For this reason, it makes sense to say that no one can have what we mean by a self unless she is disposed to identify with at least some features of her own actual past.[22]

But even if that is correct, why should someone else take my inevitable tendency to identify with my own past acts as a warrant to reward or punish me for those acts? Why should someone else be justified in acting out *my* dispositions? Wouldn't that reveal a confusion between my psychologically necessary or inevitable self-identifications and an objective metaphysical identity?

In one sense, it does seem that our commitment to other people's identification with their pasts ought to be weaker than *their* commitment to it. In another sense, however, we have the same need they do to distinguish them from the types of agent they merely exemplify; for our actual relations to them (as particular agents) play an essential role in shaping our own actual pasts, and hence our own identities. From this point of view, the point of practices like reward and punishment might be precisely to distinguish people from the types of agents they exemplify, just as their own feelings of guilt, pride, and so on enable them to distinguish themselves from those who might otherwise just as well replace them.

But perhaps there is another motive for punishment that is rather more direct than our need to individuate others in order to help us individuate ourselves. Perhaps the point is to give people (that is, force them to have) a disposition to identify with their pasts in cases where they might seem to lack that disposition. For it is not clear that my general disposition to identify with my past means that I will always do so, or do so in the right way. For instance, I might consider myself identical with the person who performed some act but fail to treat the act in question as bad; or in some cases, I might fail altogether to treat the act as still in any serious sense my own. This might be justified if, for instance, the act is one I remember performing as a child. Or I might be a criminal who fails to take his past crimes seriously because he has successfully evaded their consequences.

The point of punishment, on this account, is to force the criminal to "take responsibility for" her past acts, that is, to identify with and to respond to them appropriately. On this view we don't punish people because we believe they are in some mysterious sense metaphysically identical to the self that existed in the moment the bad act occurred— because, for instance, we literally think of them as eternally performing it. Instead, we punish them in order to make them identify with the act in a way that will *constitute* their taking responsibility for it. We do this in part because we think it is a good thing, in general, for people to identify with their pasts in ways we deem appropriate; we want them to think of themselves as having responsible selves. We want this because we want certain actions to be taken seriously, indeed with the kind of seriousness that is only possible if the agents who contemplate performing them expect the guilt or shame appropriate to such acts to become a permanent part of their own self-identification—that is, of their own attitudes toward the selves with which they will later have to identify.[23] We want to cause people, in other words, to anticipate that they will be unable to deny their identity with the selves they are when they commit whatever crime they contemplate committing.[24]

If the point of punishment is to make people anticipate that they will be unable in the future to avoid identifying with the selves they are now, then we end where we began: with the consequentialist motive of deterrence. This time, however, deterrence has been elaborated in a way that defeats the initial counterexample: we would not feel that justice had been done if an actor pretended to suffer the punishment owed a war criminal because what interests us is deterrence that proceeds not simply by way of fear but by way of each agent's disposition to take seriously the effect that his own actions will have on his future relation to himself.

If this analysis of punishment is plausible (and whether or not it is sufficient to *justify* any actual exercise of punishment—nothing said here, after all, implies that the use of punishment to force an agent to identify with her past actions is likely to *succeed*),[25] then it seems to make sense in principle to foster someone's disposition to treat herself in the present as literally answerable for certain events in the past— presumably for those events that count as actions performed by the organism she shares with the self that existed then. But if it makes sense to encourage people to take responsibility for past acts performed by the individual organisms with which they most intimately identify themselves, might it also make sense to get them to take responsibility for the acts of collectivities to which they belong? Why would it be any less rational, necessarily, to get them to experience shame or guilt, pride or pleasure, in relation to acts performed by other members of their families or classes or nations? Why not encourage them, for instance, to feel liable in some degree or other to the penalties incurred by the crimes of their ancestors? Perhaps such identifications are not psychologically necessary or inevitable in the way that identifying with at least some events in one's personal past appears to be; but it wasn't the *necessity* of the disposition that called for intervention in the case of punishment. On the contrary, punishment seemed called for precisely when a desirable identification was *not* being made. Even if there were no pre-existing disposition to identify oneself with any acts performed by someone else in a person's collective past, why not try to *create* such a disposition in order to force people to take collective guilt—and therefore collective obligations—with appropriate serious- ness? Why not try to produce persons whose attitudes toward their presently existing selves would in part be determined by their atti- tudes toward the acts performed by other members of their collectivi- ties, and whose own actions might therefore be guided in part by a desire to alleviate the guilt occasioned by the unjust acts of their ancestors?

The trouble with punishing someone for an act committed by an ancestor cannot be that he stands in a different metaphysical relation to the acts of his ancestors than he does to his own past acts. In both cases the act—as well as the state of the organism as it existed in the moment of action—is no longer present; in both cases, in other words, the justification of punishment cannot be metaphysical but can only be normative. But remember the main point of using pun- ishment to make people identify with their own actual past actions:

we do so because we want people to anticipate, as they consider performing certain acts, that the disapproval merited by those acts will become a permanent part of their own attitudes toward the selves with which they will later have to identify. The aim of punishment, on this account, is to enforce a sense of identity that can become (if not in the agent himself then in others who witness his punishment) the basis of what might be called proleptic guilt. But this requires that the act for which an agent is punished be an act that he might have avoided performing had he taken seriously enough its consequences for his later relation to himself. Yet no amount of proleptic guilt could have caused him to avoid performing an act that was never his to perform.

Punishing someone for the acts of his ancestors does not seem promising, then, as a means of giving someone a disposition to feel proleptic guilt in relation to an act he contemplates performing; on the contrary, the very notion of collective punishment involves a *separation* of accountability and action, since at least some of those held accountable are by definition not the agents who performed the reprehensible act. If anything, collective punishment may seem calculated to *weaken* an agent's disposition to connect his present actions with the self he expects to become.

Suppose, however, that what matters in the case of collective punishment is not first of all the agent's relation to her own future self but her relation to the future of her collectivity. In that case a practice of collective punishment might make sense if rationalized along the following lines: We punish someone today for an act previously performed by other members of a group to which she belongs. The punishment forces her (or others who witness it) to anticipate not that each individual will be held accountable for acts she herself performs but that, in general, members of the group will be treated— more important, will treat themselves—as if they were still performing the acts once performed by other members of the same group. Prospective wrongdoers will thus be encouraged to expect that their actions will make a permanent difference not to their *own* self-identification but to the self-identification of others who belong to the same collectivity.

Such a practice of punishment, in other words, is intended to cause an agent to anticipate, as she considers performing certain acts, that the disapproval merited by those acts will become a permanent part of the way other members of her group evaluate the selves with which they will have to identify. The point is to make her anticipate not her own guilt but the guilt that others will inherit if she acts badly. Presumably this expectation will serve as a deterrent only to the extent that the agent is inclined to feel guilty about imposing guilt on other members of her group. The logical structure of collective punishment thus turns out to be more complex than the structure of individual punishment, since it involves two distinct forms of guilt: the guilt that an agent's act will impose on others and the guilt it will impose on *her* by virtue of what it does to *them*. For that reason, the likelihood of success in the case of collective punishment may well seem more remote (one might say, *even* more remote) than in the case of individual punishment. Apart from such practical difficulties, there no doubt remain serious grounds for skepticism regarding the justice of collective punishment; above all, perhaps, it is hard to see how one might go about justifying the criteria (genetic? geographic? ideological?) by which a punishable collectivity could be defined. I will return to these difficulties later; my aim in this section has been only to determine whether the logic of punishment bears out the intuited analogy between individual and collective relations to the actual past. The foregoing analysis suggests that the answer is yes, and that the ethical relevance of the actual past in both the individual and the collective cases derives, paradoxically, from an agent's imaginative relation to the future consequences of some contemplated action. It is what we want her to imagine about the future, and not a debt owed to the past as such, that justifies, if anything does, our sense that an agent's present ethical status may properly be affected by discoveries about the actual content of her own or a collective past.

Indeed, the discovery that what matters is the agent's relation to an imagined future shows that punishment, collective or otherwise, is finally beside the point. Collective punishment, on the foregoing account, is an attempt to cause people to identify with a collective future by forcing them to identify with a collective past. What matters, for my purposes here, is not the feasibility or justice of *forcing* people to identify with a collective past but the logic of the identification as such. The central point that has emerged from this section is that the ethical relevance of the actual collective past depends on an agent's disposition to identify with an imagined collective future.

The Limits of Collective Identity

At the beginning of this chapter I advanced the presumably uncontroversial thesis that ethical and political values depend on narratives, and that shared values are likely to be connected to the narratives preserved by collective memories, whether or not such memories are embodied in a canonical literature. The question was whether the dependence of collective values on shared memories implied an equivalently strong relation to the actual (as opposed to imagined or mistakenly remembered) events of the collective past. If so, then research aimed at recovering the actual social realities suppressed by the idealized (or otherwise distorted) narratives of collective memory would have a powerful justification: it could claim to play a (necessarily and not just contingently) irreplaceable role in present political life.

The preceding sections have addressed this question in two very different ways: first, by analyzing the rhetoric of certain programmatic statements by scholars engaged in revisionist research; second, by exploring the logic of a practice that necessarily depends on the assumption that present agents are, or ought to be, inescapably bound to the actual past. The results so far have been mixed. One way of establishing the relevance of the actual collective past indeed proved untenable; the fact that a past phenomenon might both resemble and help to explain a present phenomenon proved insufficient to give the past any intrinsic claim on present action. On the other hand, the analysis of punishment uncovered a way in which it might make sense, at least in principle, to encourage people to think of themselves as inheriting the guilt or shame (or merit or obligations) created by what actually happened in a collective past. What remains to be seen is how this second outcome bears on the chief concern of this chapter, namely, the ethical or political relevance of revisionism.

If the analysis of collective punishment was correct, then it seems possible for a present agent to stand in the same relation to actions performed by other agents as she stands in relation to actions performed by the self "she" earlier was. Since what finally matters in ascriptions of responsibility for past actions is the self's disposition to identify with the consequences of its future actions, neither organic identity (continuity of body) nor psychological identity (continuity of memory) seems to be a necessary condition of responsibility. If this is true, there is no reason to deny that an agent might have the same kind of ethical interest in discoveries about her collective past as an amnesiac would have in discoveries about forgotten events in her personal history. She might be more than curious, wanting to know what punishment or reward she unwittingly deserves, or what forgotten obligation she ought to fulfill. Perhaps we should think of the readership of revisionist inquiry as a collection of amnesiacs, each awaiting the next disclosure with an appropriate mixture of excitement and dread.

At this point, however, the special difficulties associated with collective punishment begin to reassert themselves. Remember, first of all, that the rationale of collective punishment involves a desire to make an agent consider what his own actions might do to the ethical status of other members of his collectivity. But this will only work if he cares about *their* future identity in the same way that he may be expected to care about his own. There is of course no guarantee that he will care very much about the future in either case, but at least in the case of his own identity we can fall back on the fact that *some* tendency to identify with one's own past and future seems built into the structure of human agency. That may be one reason why it seems difficult to imagine that an amnesiac might be simply indifferent to information about his past identity, while there is something slightly comical about the image of a scholarly readership eagerly awaiting new disclosures about crimes in the collective past.

The trouble with collective identifications across time, however, is not simply that they may be less inevitably made or intimately felt than identifications with the organism's own past and future states. Another difficulty lies in the fact that they are far easier to *deny*.[26] This problem emerged earlier in the form of a question about the justice of collective punishment given the absence of clear criteria as to what should count as a punishable collectivity. But its implications extend beyond the perhaps anomalous case of collective punishment to other, less peculiar expressions of collective responsibility. Consider, for example, the notion of collective accountability recently defended by Alasdair MacIntyre in the course of an eloquent attack on the ideology of individualism. After observing, incontrovertibly, that "we all approach our own circumstances as bearers of a particular social identity," MacIntyre makes the somewhat stronger claim that "I inherit from the past of my family, my city, my tribe, my nation, a variety of debts, inheritances, rightful expectations and obligations." "This thought," he acknowledges, is likely to appear alien and even surprising from the standpoint of modern individualism. From the standpoint of individualism I am what I myself choose to be. I can always, if I wish to, put in question what are taken to be the merely contingent social features of my existence. I may biologically be my father's son; but I cannot be held responsible for what he did unless I choose implicitly or explicitly to assume such responsibility. I may legally be a citizen of a certain country; but I cannot be held responsible for what my country does or has done unless I choose . . . to assume such responsibility. Such individualism is expressed by those modern Americans who deny any responsibility for the effects of slavery upon black Americans, saying "I never owned any slaves." It is more subtly the standpoint of those other modern Americans who accept a nicely calculated responsibility for such effects measured precisely by the benefits they themselves as individuals have indirectly received from slavery. In both cases 'being an American' is not in itself taken to be part of the moral identity of the individual. And of course there is nothing peculiar to modern Americans in this attitude: the Englishman who says, "*I* never did any wrong to Ireland; why bring up that old history as though it had something to do with *me?*" or the young German who believes that being born after 1945 means that what Nazis did to Jews has no moral relevance to his relationship to his Jewish contemporaries, exhibit the same attitude, that according to which the self is detachable from its social and historical roles and statuses.[27]

MacIntyre's irony toward the liberal assumption that guilt for collective crimes is somehow voluntary is no doubt justified. What interests me at the moment, however, is not the cogency of MacIntyre's attack on liberalism but a curious inconsistency in his account of collective guilt. Modern Americans, according to MacIntyre, should acknowledge responsibility for the effects of slavery not when they feel so inclined or to the extent that they have individually benefited from it but simply insofar as they belong to the American collectivity and thus partake of an American identity. But if "modern Americans" automatically inherit this morally tainted collective identity, should we conclude that modern "*black* Americans" inherit it as well? Or do the disadvantages of belonging to the collectivity "black America" cancel out the guilt that one would otherwise inherit as a member of the collectivity "America"? To say that disadvantages can outweigh collective guilt is presumably to exhibit the same sort of "nice calculation" that MacIntyre perceives in Americans who measure their guilt for slavery by the benefits they have received from it. But what alternative does MacIntyre's argument allow? If present benefits and ongoing injuries are beside the point, if collective guilt for the past is taken seriously in its own right and is not just a figurative way of referring to present inequities, then it is hard to see why modern African-Americans are any less responsible for the effects of slavery than Americans generally. Are "black Americans" themselves thus guilty for "the effects of slavery upon black Americans"?[28]

The dilemma posed by MacIntyre's account merely dramatizes a general weakness, at least in modern liberal societies, of ascriptions of (morally significant) collective identity. The difficulty can be stated succinctly: collective identities, unlike individual ones, frequently overlap. In this sense the voluntarism MacIntyre criticizes as a product of liberal individualism merely describes a feature of large-scale collectivities as such. Citizens born into a nation that has committed crimes can always claim innocence based on their membership in additional collectivities: not just an American but a black American, or a recent immigrant; not just a German but a socialist, a European, a Christian, an intellectual. Of course there is no guarantee that an agent will *succeed* in disowning collective guilt by denying that the collectivity in question defines her identity or determines her ethical status more powerfully than does some other collectivity to which she also belongs. No doubt there are cultural situations in which membership in one collectivity—for example, clan membership in a tribal society or early Christian membership in the "body of Christ"—counts as sufficiently important to render competing memberships negligible by comparison.[29] In such cases it may even be easier, thanks to initiation or conversion, for an agent to repudiate her personal past than it is for her to deny her connection to the past of the collectivity. Hence the problem of deniability, though possibly intractable in our present social context, does not amount to a logically necessary obstacle to all practices of binding people to actual events in their collective pasts.

Perhaps the reconstructive tendency in literary-historical scholarship should be understood, then, precisely as an attempt to restore a pre-liberal mode of identity, so that membership in some specified collectivity will once again override the plurality of identifications that tends, in our present context, to defeat ascriptions of collective responsibility. (Something like this is what Schüssler Fiorenza seems to envision when she calls, in a passage cited earlier, for "a universal solidarity of sisterhood with all women of the past, present, and future who follow the same vision"; *MH,* p. 31.)

But if this is a plausible way to construe an important aim of reconstructive scholarship, then such scholarship may in many cases turn out to be curiously self-defeating. For a central tendency of current research designed to replace collective memories with an account of the actual past is surely to *multiply* the grounds for denying collective identity of the sort that seems necessary for ascriptions of collective responsibility in the strong sense we have been exploring. If collective identity of the pre-liberal sort is based, at least to an important extent, on the possession of common narratives, whatever undermines those narratives will inevitably tend to qualify, even if it does not destroy, one's sense of belonging to the collectivity whose past has been revised. In general, the pre-critical narratives that connect us to a collective past tend to presuppose that our ancestors largely shared our beliefs and values, for only in that case can our actions readily be seen as continuations of theirs. Suppose, recalling an example from an earlier section, that a modern American accepts a responsibility to promote egalitarianism because he believes that he has inherited this obligation from his colonial ancestors. Presumably he does so in part because of an assumption derived from certain collective narratives: the assumption that these ancestors understood egalitarianism in roughly the way he understands it. He now learns, by reading Edmund S. Morgan's account, that a crucial component of what they meant by egalitarianism was slaveholding. Nothing in principle prevents him from simply embracing this information as a discovery about the true content of his inherited obligation, and thus from taking up the banner of slavery. But a more likely outcome would seem to be uncertainty that a transhistorical American identity—and thus a body of inherited American obligations—really existed in quite the way he used to think.

The Relevance of Historical Revision

The burden of this chapter has been skeptical. My reflections have tended, on the whole, to raise doubts about the intrinsic ethical or political importance of new discoveries about what actually took place "behind" the narratives preserved in collective memory. Indeed, my arguments so far might plausibly be taken to imply that I consider research into the background of canonical narratives ethically and politically irrelevant—mere antiquarianism, in Jameson's sense. The purpose of this section is consequently to point to several ways in which such research might indeed prove relevant to present values, even if not quite for the reasons imagined by the critics treated in the opening sections.

My argument to this point has assumed that people's ethical and political values take the form of commitments to doctrines or images that are in turn dependent on imagined or remembered patterns of action. Suppose it turns out, however, that at least some ethical values held by some people involve commitments not to a pattern of action but to *whatever actually occurred* in some designated segment of the past or *whatever was actually done* by some designated ancestor. Suppose, in other words, that the logic of ethical values is at least sometimes *indexical,* so that a disposition to act in an ethically appropriate way is a disposition to act in the way some designated person or group acted, whatever that may have been.[30] Thus a religious believer of a certain kind might be disposed to act in the way a particular saint acted, whatever the saint's actions turned out to have been and whether or not they matched the received accounts. In that case, a historical discovery that revised the traditional record of the saint's actions would *necessarily* change the content of the believer's values, and nothing else could change it in the same way. Presumably there would be a limit to how far revision could go before the believer repudiated the value of acting in whatever way the saint acted—for instance, if the historical reconstruction showed that the saint was a murderer. The limit in this case would be set by the other values, perhaps non-indexical ones, to which the believer was also committed. Nevertheless, whether or not the believer remained committed to the value of imitating the saint, the content of that value would have changed, necessarily, along with the historical information.

The question is whether anyone's values really take this "indexical" form—that is, the form of a commitment to act in whatever way it turns out that some designated person acted, or perhaps an intention to mean by some ethical term whatever some designated ancestors meant by it. Might there really be, for instance, an American whose commitment to "equality" was in fact a commitment to whatever the Founders meant when they affirmed it? Possibly there is no one whose ethical dispositions could be understood primarily in these terms, though *some* degree of indexical commitment may play a role in the normative life of any agent or collectivity.

The second kind of relevance I have in mind is less interesting theoretically (since it stops short of giving discoveries about the past a *necessary* relevance to the present) but perhaps more plausible psychologically as an account of how someone might be affected by reconstructive inquiry. Suppose one discovers that a value one presently holds has been linked in the past to motives or consequences that now seem repulsive; suppose this discovery creates a suspicion that the value in question is still linked to something one would like to repudiate. (Conversely, research might show that a value one no longer holds has been linked to benefits one still finds attractive, and this might lead one to ask whether the neglected value deserves a revival.) Perhaps, once again, I am convinced by Morgan's claim that the notion of equality was connected in colonial Virginia to a slaveholding ideology. As has been suggested, this is unlikely to persuade me to revise my concept of egalitarianism along colonial Virginian lines. But I might begin to wonder whether egalitarian advocacy in certain contexts in the present might not end up serving similar ends, for instance by reinforcing the solidarity of one group at the expense of another.

The fact that someone might be led to question his present commitments in this way would not show that historical research was necessary to the correction or more careful application of present values, since the potentially oppressive consequences of his egalitarian values could in principle have been demonstrated by fictional examples or by logical analysis. Still, it was useful, and in practice may have been invaluable, to have the historical precedent to work with; novelists and political theorists might never have invented an equally revealing example. In this sense, historical investigation of the origins of present values may serve as a means of gathering examples that provoke reflection on the possible social consequences of certain ideological commitments, though, once again, there would be no necessary connection between the historical actuality of the example and its utility. In fact, the historicity of the example might be positively misleading, if for instance the alleged status of the Virginia ideology as the true historical origin of American egalitarianism were interpreted (via genetic fallacy) to mean that the connection between egalitarianism and oppression was a necessary one.[31]

The last kind of relevance I wish to mention has less to do with information than with motivation. In the previous section, I imagined a reader of Morgan's history who began to wonder whether an American identity really existed in quite the way he or she had previously thought. To say, however, that such a discovery might raise questions about the precise character of an American identity is not to say that the reader's commitment to what she perceived as American values would therefore be weakened. On the contrary, recognizing the fragility and contingency of American egalitarianism in its earliest moments might intensify one's sense of an obligation to preserve and foster this inherited value, despite or even because of its ambiguous lineage.

Conclusion

What are we to make, finally, of the kind of project explored in Chapter 5—in the most general terms, the project of connecting (or reconnecting) people to the actual? Is it, for one thing, a formalist or an anti-formalist project? Is it like or unlike the avowedly formalist activity of focusing one's attention on a symbol that "absorbs the interest of its referents into itself"?[1] Ostensibly, to shift attention from a work's imaginative structure to the actual material circumstances of its production (from *Isabella,* say, to the economic realities of early nineteenth-century Britain) is to perform an *anti*-formalist gesture. In performing that act (again, ostensibly), one forbids oneself (and others) the irresponsible pleasures of what Keats called "speculation."

And yet the imperative to attend to the actual, whether understood as a psychological, an ethical, or a political necessity, involves a logic that is remarkably akin to the logic of the "concrete universal," as that notion was analyzed and (partly) defended in Chapter 3. For it turns out, on the analysis in Chapter 5, that I can only conceive myself as a *particular* agent—can only distinguish myself from others with whom I share the same possibility of future action—if I conceive myself not just as causally linked to my actual past but as bound in some irreducible way to whatever happened in it. But at the same time, I can only conceive myself as an *agent* if I can deliberate about my possible future acts (including whatever acts are supposed to flow from my engagement with the actual). And that means reflecting on what it is appropriate for someone in my situation to do, which in turn involves conceiving myself as an example of a certain *type* of agent, in a certain *type* of situation. I have to see myself, in other words, as in principle replaceable by any other agent who might share my values and opportunities.

Its role as an agent, or its aspiring to that role, thus gives the self a peculiarly double status as replaceable example and irreplaceable singularity. From this point of view, the self actually *is* a concrete universal, or makes itself so by identifying with the particular events and objects that, in another sense, it can always leave behind (*has* always left behind). The self, in other words, is a formalist, and never more so than when it attempts to escape its formalism by binding itself still more strictly to what particularizes it.[2] Hence the persistence, and the persistent irony, of anti-formalism.

But if formalism is built into our conception of ourselves as agents, what does that say about the specific mode of formalism associated with what I have been calling literary interest? Does it at last suggest a way, for instance, to give literary interest an intrinsic ethical relevance, despite the skeptical considerations in Chapters 2 and 4?

At least we are now in a position to spell out the analogy between literary structures and our practical self-conceptions more precisely than in earlier chapters. My self-conception as an agent requires me to imagine myself as essentially bound to my particular past, while at the same time continuing to see myself as confronted by the choices open to a certain *type* of agent, a type of which I am only one (replaceable) example.[3] Literary works particularize the typical meanings and values of their objects by inserting those objects, together with their typical responses, into new composite networks of association. In neither case is the fusion of particularity and typicality fully achievable. For in both cases the typical can only be particularized at the cost of diminishing its typicality; and, also in both cases, the particular is haunted by the irreducible typicality of the elements it conjoins. Regicide in *Macbeth* is no longer typical regicide; but rooks and woods can only modify it if they retain their typical associations. Similarly, an actual murderer's possibilities of future action are reduced by the insistence, which even he must share, that his future be determined by at least some consequences of his actual past. But he can only understand the past to which he binds himself if he can evaluate his own past acts, and he can only do *that* if he understands those acts as possibilities that were once available to a certain *type* of agent. For otherwise they would have lacked the intentional structure of specifiable actions; they would merely have been unintelligible events that happened to befall him.[4]

In Chapter 4 I suggested that literary interest provided an unusually pure experience of what it was like to be an agent, at least as agency is conceived in a certain broad tradition of "liberal" thought. We are now in a position to go beyond the historicism of that suggestion, by adding that literary interest offers an unusually precise and concentrated analogue of what it is like to be an agent in general. For part of what being an agent is (always) like, apparently, is being caught up in an irreducible oscillation between typicality and particularity: between (on one side) the forms of action that an agent must understand in order to make sense of herself as the possible performer of certain actions, and (on the other side) the concrete history without which the agent could not distinguish herself from those who might, otherwise, just as well replace her. And this, once again, resembles the structure of mutual implication that characterizes the relation between the typicality of literary object-types and the particularity of the complex scenarios in which the literary work inserts them.

But why would anyone want to experience a "precise and concentrated" analogue of what being an agent is like? What might this add to the ordinary experience of simply being, or trying to be, an agent? Possibly nothing; after all, the mere fact that two phenomena are analogous doesn't show that the analogy plays any role in motivating people's interest in either one. There is no sure way to deduce a psychological interest from this sort of structural possibility. The most one can venture is a speculation, one that cannot be reliably grounded in logical analysis, and equally one that no empirical survey of people's multifarious responses to literary artifacts could hope to confirm.

Here, then, is a speculative answer. From one point of view, the mutual implication of particularity and typicality that characterizes the structure of literary interest merely reproduces the oscillation that also characterizes the self-reflection of human agency. At best (from this standpoint) it might be said to provide a clear demonstration of why this oscillation is permanent, and therefore why these two aspects of our construing ourselves as agents must continue to operate, even if they do so at each other's expense. For what makes the literary artifact "literary," in the sense I have been developing, is precisely the way its typical elements are particularized by their insertion into a structure whose tendency toward full concreteness they nevertheless frustrate.

And yet the very structure of mutual implication that reveals the impossibility of ultimately fusing particularity and typicality may continue to tantalize us with the promise of fusing them; or at least of fusing them, as we say, for all *practical* purposes. Since that promise is also the promise of full agency as we are (practically) committed to conceiving it, it may not be surprising, finally, if encountering its literary version should feel like glimpsing the ideal condition of practical agency itself.

NOTES

INDEX

Notes

Introduction

1. For a relatively early but still impressive diagnosis of literary formalism as an institutional and political ideology, see Richard Ohmann, *English in America: A Radical View of the Profession* (New York: Oxford University Press, 1976). A more careful version of the historical case for an ideological interpretation of New Criticism and other varieties of American formalism is provided by Gerald Graff, *Professing Literature: An Institutional History* (Chicago: University of Chicago Press, 1987), chs. 9–14.
2. Steven Knapp, *Personification and the Sublime: Milton to Coleridge* (Cambridge, Mass.: Harvard University Press, 1985).
3. Throughout this study I will be using the term "theoretical" in a broader and weaker sense than the one usually at issue in recent debates about the status of "theory" in literary criticism. For a definition of theory in the broad, weak sense, see Graff, *Professing Literature,* p. 252. For an argument against theory in the stronger and narrower sense (and *only* in that sense), see Steven Knapp and Walter Benn Michaels, "Against Theory," *Critical Inquiry,* 8 (Summer 1982), 723–742, rpt. in *Against Theory: Literary Studies and the New Pragmatism,* ed. W. J. T. Mitchell (Chicago: University of Chicago Press, 1985), pp. 11–30; see also in the Mitchell volume Stanley Fish, "Consequences," pp. 106–131.
4. My distinction between interpretive and literary interest roughly parallels the distinction between "verbal meaning" and "significance" long ago proposed by E. D. Hirsch; see *Validity in Interpretation* (New Haven: Yale University Press, 1967), p. 8 and passim. My adoption of a version

of Hirsch's distinction does not, however, imply a commitment to the methodological project with which Hirsch himself, at least in his early writings, associated it.

5. For an influential example of this increasingly wide-spread tendency, see Alasdair MacIntyre, *After Virtue: A Study in Moral Theory,* 2nd ed. (Notre Dame: University of Notre Dame Press, 1984), ch. 15.

1. Authorial Action and the Worlds of *Paradise Lost*

1. Blake's remarks on Milton are conveniently brought together in *The Romantics on Milton: Formal Essays and Critical Asides,* ed. Joseph Anthony Wittreich, Jr. (Cleveland: Press of Case Western University, 1970), pp. 33–97. The remark quoted here, from *The Marriage of Heaven and Hell* (ca. 1790–1793), appears on p. 35.

2. A. J. A. Waldock, *"Paradise Lost" and Its Critics* (Cambridge: Cambridge University Press, 1947), p. 144. For the view that the unattractiveness of Milton's God is an unavoidable consequence of Milton's formal intentions, see Ralph W. Rader, "Fact, Theory and Literary Explanation," *Critical Inquiry,* 1 (1974–1975), 266–269. A full treatment of the rhetorical version of the Romantic critique would involve reopening the modern debate over Milton's style; for a critical review of the relevant issues, see Paul J. Alpers, "The Milton Controversy," in *Twentieth-Century Literature in Retrospect,* Harvard English Studies 2, ed. Reuben A. Brower (Cambridge, Mass.: Harvard University Press, 1971), pp. 269–298.

3. For one of numerous versions of this account, see Christine Froula, "When Eve Reads Milton: Undoing the Canonical Economy," *Critical Inquiry,* 10 (December 1983), 321–347.

4. Steven Knapp and Walter Benn Michaels, "Against Theory 2: Hermeneutics and Deconstruction," *Critical Inquiry,* 14 (Autumn 1987), 49–68; see also "Against Theory," *Critical Inquiry,* 8 (Summer 1982), 723–742, rpt. in *Against Theory: Literary Studies and the New Pragmatism,* ed. W. J. T. Mitchell (Chicago: University of Chicago Press, 1985), pp. 11–30.

5. My terminology here follows the account of "world projection" given by Nicholas Wolterstorff in *Worlds and Works of Art* (Oxford: Clarendon, 1980), especially pts. 3 and 4; hereafter abbreviated as *WWA.* For a comprehensive attempt to base a theory of literary fiction on recent philosophical work on the logical status of imagined "worlds," see Thomas G. Pavel, *Fictional Worlds* (Cambridge, Mass.: Harvard University Press, 1986). Pavel, however, does not directly address the issue of the authorial action involved in projecting a fictional world.

In drawing on Wolterstorff's notion of world projection, I am not concerned to defend or criticize the details of his elaborate and often highly technical argument. Nor am I endorsing the particular metaphysical position—a version of what David Lewis has called "modal realism"—that Wolterstorff takes his theory to presuppose. (See David Lewis, *On the Plurality of Worlds* [Oxford: Basil Blackwell, 1986], p. viii.) For my purposes, it makes no difference whether, for instance, a state of affairs that is imagined but not actual can be said to "exist." (According to Wolterstorff [*WWA*, p. 127], all states of affairs *exist,* including impossible ones, but only some states of affairs *occur.*) It makes no difference, furthermore, whether imaginary states of affairs are, as Wolterstorff supposes, necessarily subject to the rules of logic that apply to the relations between states of affairs in the actual world. It does not matter, in short, whether there are such things as projected *worlds* in precisely Wolterstorff's sense. All that matters is that it be possible for an author to project a world whose states of affairs can be *treated* as subject to logical analysis and evaluation.

6. Percy Bysshe Shelley, *A Defence of Poetry* (1821), in Wittreich, *The Romantics on Milton,* p. 537.

7. Ibid., pp. 537–538; see also the closely related excerpt from *On the Devil, and Devils,* p. 535.

8. *Milton's God,* 3rd ed. (Cambridge: Cambridge University Press, 1981), p. 181; first edition published in 1961. For Empson's qualified endorsement of Shelley's position, see pp. 13–21. Shelley's only mistake, according to Empson, was to suppose "that Milton secretly despised the popular myths which were the material of his art" (pp. 15–16).

9. Here again the theory I am following is essentially that of Wolterstorff (see note 5). Wolterstorff's account of fiction has been strongly criticized, along with several other speech-act accounts, by Kendall L. Walton in "Fiction, Fiction-Making, and Styles of Fictionality," *Philosophy and Literature,* 7 (1983), 78–88; see also Walton's detailed review of Wolterstorff's book in *The Journal of Philosophy,* 80 (1983), 179–193. For a comprehensive statement of Walton's own theory, repeating his criticisms of Wolterstorff et al., see his *Mimesis as Make-Believe: On the Foundations of the Representational Arts* (Cambridge, Mass.: Harvard University Press, 1990).

According to Walton, "a work of fiction is a prop in a game of make-believe of a certain sort, a game played by appreciators"; any actions involved in the *making* of such props are irrelevant to their "role in appreciators' activities" ("Fiction," p. 87). Even natural objects—"rock patterns and clouds" (p. 86)—can be used by appreciators to generate fictional worlds. If Walton is right, then it follows (trivially) that the world of a fictional "work" is never, except by accident, the world projected by authorial action. This is not, however, the place to engage Walton's analysis of fiction; the possibility that appreciators of *Paradise Lost* might be indifferent to the world Milton intended to project is irrelevant to the question of what that world was and whether he succeeded in projecting it.

10. *WWA,* pp. 131–132. Someone who rejects Wolterstorff's modal realism will presumably deny that there are such things as "maximally comprehensive" possible worlds and will thus consider this distinction between projected and possible worlds superfluous.

The incompleteness of fictional worlds has become a central issue in discussions of the ontological status of fiction; see, for example, Marie-Laure Ryan, "Fiction as Logical, Ontological, and Illocutionary Issue" (a review of Felix Martínez-Bonati, *Fictive Discourse and the Structures of Literature*), *Style,* 18 (1984), 129–134; see also Pavel, *Fictional Worlds,* pp. 105–113. Wolterstorff's full treatment of this issue involves an elaborate and perhaps eccentric account of the ontology of fictional characters (*WWA,* 134–163).

11. Cf. Michael Dummett, *The Logical Basis of Metaphysics* (Cambridge, Mass.: Harvard University Press, 1991), p. 318: "If our statements and our thoughts are not all determinately either true or false, then reality itself is indeterminate; it has gaps, much as a novel has gaps, in that there are questions about the characters to which the novel provides no answers, and to which there therefore are no answers."

12. For a discussion of eighteenth- and twentieth-century responses to Milton's inclusion of impossible states of affairs in the world of *Paradise Lost,* see Steven Knapp, *Personification and the Sublime: Milton to Coleridge* (Cambridge, Mass.: Harvard University Press, 1985), ch. 2 and Epilogue, respectively.

13. *Paradise Lost,* Book II, line 989, in *The Poems of John Milton,* ed. John Carey and Alastair Fowler (London: Longman, 1968, and New York: Norton, 1972), p. 554. Subsequent references to *Paradise Lost* will be to this edition and will be given in the text by book and line.

14. He could not, however, have been a philosophical atheist, at least not of the standard kind, since a belief that theism was *necessarily* false would have precluded his intending to project a world in which it was true. (According to Wolterstorff, incidentally, we ought to have "a sharp sense for the difference between a state of affairs' being true in some projected world and its being true in our actual world" [*WWA,* p. 110]. But I have not adopted his terminological proposal that we henceforth speak of a proposition or a state of affairs not as "*true* in some work's world, but only as *included within* it." I will speak instead of a state of affairs or a proposition in a projected world *counting* as true or being *putatively* true.)

15. *Christian Doctrine,* ed. Maurice Kelley, trans. John Carey, in *Complete Prose Works of John Milton,* ed. Don M. Wolfe et al. (New Haven: Yale University Press, 1973), VI, 165.

16. Anthony Kenny, *The God of the Philosophers* (Oxford: Clarendon, 1979), pp. 79–83; Alvin Plantinga, *God, Freedom, and Evil* (New York: Harper and Row, 1974), pp. 66–72. Plantinga is responding to Nelson Pike, "Divine Omniscience and Voluntary Action," *Philosophical Review,* 74 (1965), 27–46; Pike replied in "Divine Foreknowledge, Human Freedom, and Possible Worlds," *Philosophical Review,* 86 (1977), 209–216. For a recent analysis of the debate between Pike and Plantinga (with a conclusion in favor of Plantinga), see Philip L. Quinn, "Plantinga on Foreknowledge and Freedom," in *Alvin Plantinga,* ed. James E. Tomberlin and Peter van Inwagen (Dordrecht: D. Reidel, 1985), pp. 271–287.

   Dennis Richard Danielson discusses the problem of foreknowledge and freedom in the course of his comprehensive treatment of Milton's relation to the various logical issues raised by theodicy; see *Milton's Good God: A Study in Literary Theodicy* (Cambridge: Cambridge University Press, 1982), pp. 154–163. See also R. D. Bedford, "Time, Freedom, and Foreknowledge in *Paradise Lost,*" *Milton Studies,* 16 (1982), 61–76.

17. Alvin Plantinga, *The Nature of Necessity* (Oxford: Clarendon, 1974), pp. 184–189; the same argument appears in Plantinga, *God, Freedom, and Evil,* pp. 45–63. Plantinga's argument is discussed by Danielson, *Milton's Good God,* p. 94.

18. *Alvin Plantinga,* ed. Tomberlin and van Inwagen, pp. 405–406.

19. For a full statement of the case against attributing to Milton any degree of belief in a "fortunate Fall," see Danielson, *Milton's Good God,* ch. 7. Danielson's view is representative of recent criticism on this issue, but the growing consensus has in one respect been challenged by Diana Benet in "Satan, God's Glory and the Fortunate Fall," *Milton Quarterly,* 19 (1985), 34–37. According to Benet, God's responses to the Fall inevitably augment his own glory, even if his creatures would have been better off without it.

20. Cf. Robert M[erihew] Adams, "Plantinga on the Problem of Evil," in *Alvin Plantinga,* ed. Tomberlin and van Inwagen, pp. 251–252.

21. Cf. Donald Davidson: "Hobbes, Locke, Hume, Moore, Schlick, Ayer, Stevenson, and a host of others have done what can be done, or ought ever to have been needed, to remove the confusions that can make determinism seem to frustrate freedom" (*Essays on Actions and Events* [Oxford: Clarendon, 1980], p. 63). Despite this confident assertion, compatibilism continues to have its challengers; for a recent example see Peter van Inwagen, *An Essay on Free Will* (Oxford: Clarendon, 1983). For equally

energetic arguments on the compatibilist side, see Daniel C. Dennett, *Elbow Room: The Varieties of Free Will Worth Having* (Cambridge, Mass.: MIT Press, 1984). Libertarianism and compatibilism are not, however, the only options. For skeptical reflections on both views, see Thomas Nagel, *The View from Nowhere* (New York: Oxford University Press, 1986), ch. 7.

22. *Christian Doctrine,* pp. 161–162. Danielson uses this passage, along with numerous sources from Milton and his contemporaries, to develop a decisive argument against modern attempts to turn Milton into a compatibilist; see *Milton's Good God,* pp. 132–149. He stops short of explaining, however, how Milton's libertarianism can survive the standard philosophical objections or how the *poem* can survive its failure to do so.

23. A. J. Ayer, "Freedom and Necessity," in *Free Will,* ed. Gary Watson (New York: Oxford University Press, 1982), p. 18. Ayer's article is reprinted from his *Philosophical Essays* (London: Macmillan, 1954), pp. 271–284. J. B. Savage applies Ayer's argument to Milton's epic in "Freedom and Necessity in *Paradise Lost,*" ELH, 44 (1977), 290.

24. Cf. Gary Watson, Introduction, in *Free Will,* ed. Watson, p. 10.

25. Roderick M. Chisholm, "Freedom and Action," in *Freedom and Determinism,* ed. Keith Lehrer (New York: Random House, 1966), p. 23.

26. For an argument that prior mental states contribute to free actions without determining them, see van Inwagen, *An Essay on Free Will,* pp. 151–152.

27. For a related objection, see Bernard Williams's Lindley Lecture, *How Free Does the Will Need to Be?* (Lawrence, Kans.: Department of Philosophy, University of Kansas, 1986), pp. 5–7.

28. Cf. Stanley Eugene Fish, *Surprised by Sin: The Reader in "Paradise Lost,"* 2nd ed. (Berkeley and Los Angeles: University of California Press, 1971), p. 240: "The unintelligibility, and hence the freedom, of the transition [from sinlessness to sin] is Milton's thesis. Making it intelligible, and hence excusable . . . is the reader's temptation."

29. In other words, each impossible state of affairs can be replaced by its "conjunctive analysis," that is, can be broken down into a "set of distinct states of affairs," at least some of which are possible and can be used to "ground extrapolation"; see Wolterstorff, *WWA,* p. 119.

30. On the role of "extrapolation" in reconstructing the world "projected" by a work of art, see Wolterstorff, *WWA,* pp. 116–124.

31. The claim that the poem makes sense only if we stipulate that God is a liar plays a prominent role in Empson's argument; see, for example, *Milton's God,* pp. 41–42, 145–146.

32. For convenient summaries of some of the relevant Gnostic doctrines, see

Hans Jonas, *The Gnostic Religion: The Message of the Alien God and the Beginnings of Christianity,* 2nd ed. (Boston: Beacon Press, 1963), pp. 42–44, 132–136, 141–143, 190–194.

33. Empson, *Milton's God,* pp. 143–144; for other respects in which Milton's God resembles, according to Empson, "the God of the Gnostics," see pp. 85–88.

34. Ibid., p. 322.

35. For a related critique of the notion of "supplementing" an author's intended meaning, see Knapp and Michaels, "Against Theory 2"; see also Steven Knapp, "Practice, Purpose, and Interpretive Controversy," in *Pragmatism in Law and Society,* ed. Michael Brint and William Weaver (Boulder, Colo.: Westview, 1991), pp. 323–342.

2. Negative Capability

1. *The Letters of John Keats,* ed. Hyder Edward Rollins, 2 vols. (Cambridge, Mass.: Harvard University Press, 1958), I, 192. Further references to Keats's letters will be to this edition, cited in the text as *Letters,* followed by volume and page number.

2. An implicit identification of "negative capability" and "disinterestedness" informs the otherwise careful account of Keats's ideas by Walter Jackson Bate in *John Keats* (Cambridge, Mass.: Harvard University Press, 1963); see especially ch. 10. See also Bate's earlier study, *Negative Capability: The Intuitive Approach in Keats* (Cambridge, Mass.: Harvard University Press, 1939). My own reading of Keats's letters, however, tends to confirm the judgment of Margaret Ann Fitzpatrick that, for Keats, "imagination and disinterestedness are quite distinct. Keats's use of the word 'distinterestedness' seems to be always associated with the world of active benevolence rather than with art" ("The Problem of 'Identity' in Keats's 'Negative Capability,' " *Dalhousie Review,* 61 [Spring 1981], 41). Fitzpatrick plausibly argues that the standard reading rests on a conflation of Keats's views and Hazlitt's.

3. Bate, *John Keats,* p. 636.

4. Quotations of Keats's *Isabella,* identified in the text by line number only, will be taken from *The Poems of John Keats,* ed. Jack Stillinger (Cambridge, Mass.: Harvard University Press, 1978).

5. Stillinger, ed., *Poems of John Keats,* p. 503.

6. Claude Lee Finney, *The Evolution of Keats's Poetry,* 2 vols. (Cambridge, Mass.: Harvard University Press, 1936), I, 374.

7. Keats's ambiguous use of the word in *Isabella* thus reinforces Susan Wolfson's observation that "throughout the poem, literary and commercial riches, literary taste and commercial venture, wind up on the

same axis of imagery"; see Wolfson, "Keats's *Isabella* and the 'Digressions' of 'Romance,'" *Criticism,* 27 (Summer 1985), 247–261. For a comprehensive reading of the poem's economic themes and imagery in relation to "the politics of its composition and the economics of its literary reception," see Kurt Heinzelman, "Self-Interest and the Politics of Composition in Keats's *Isabella,*" *ELH,* 55 (Spring 1988), 159–193.

8. John Middleton Murry, *Keats,* 4th ed. (New York: Noonday, 1955), p. 227.

9. Ibid., p. 228.

10. Immanuel Kant, *Critique of Judgment,* trans. J. H. Bernard (New York: Hafner, 1951), p. 157; hereafter cited in the text as *CJ.*

11. See Immanuel Kant, *Critique of Pure Reason,* trans. Norman Kemp Smith (New York: St. Martin's Press, 1965), p. 65: "The capacity (receptivity) for receiving representations through the mode in which we are affected by objects, is entitled *sensibility.* Objects are *given* to us by means of sensibility, and it alone yields us *intuitions;* they are *thought* through the understanding, and from the understanding arise *concepts.* But all thought must, directly or indirectly, by way of certain characters, relate ultimately to intuitions, and therefore, with us, to sensibility, because in no other way can an object be given to us" (A 19).

12. John Hodgson, *Coleridge, Shelley, and Transcendental Inquiry* (Lincoln: University of Nebraska Press, 1989), pp. 12–14.

13. Janet Martin Soskice, *Metaphor and Religious Language* (Oxford: Clarendon, 1985), p. 134.

14. Donald Davidson, "What Metaphors Mean," in *Inquiries into Truth and Interpretation* (Oxford: Clarendon, 1984), pp. 245–264; hereafter cited as "WMM." The quoted phrase appears on page 262. In the course of his essay, Davidson criticizes earlier accounts of metaphor by Richards, Black, Goodman, Barfield, and others, but this is not the occasion to give Davidson's account a precise location within the context of modern theories. For a concise survey of recent theories, though from a perspective unsympathetic to Davidson's, see George Lakoff and Mark Turner, *More than Cool Reason: A Field Guide to Poetic Metaphor* (Chicago: University of Chicago Press, 1989), pp. 110–136, 217–218.

15. Soskice, *Metaphor,* pp. 30–31.

16. Max Black, "How Metaphors Work: A Reply to Donald Davidson," in *On Metaphor,* ed. Sheldon Sacks (Chicago: University of Chicago Press, 1979), p. 184n; quoted by Soskice, *Metaphor,* p. 30.

17. Dan Sperber and Deirdre Wilson, *Relevance: Communication and Cognition* (Cambridge, Mass.: Harvard University Press, 1986); hereafter cited as *Relevance.*

18. For a fuller indication of what Sperber and Wilson mean by "poetic," see *Relevance*, pp. 217–224.

3. The Concrete Universal

1. W. K. Wimsatt, Jr., *The Verbal Icon: Studies in the Meaning of Poetry* (Lexington: University Press of Kentucky, 1954), 273; hereafter abbreviated as *VI* and cited parenthetically in the text.

2. *Longinus on the Sublime*, trans. W. R. Roberts (1899); rpt. in *Critical Theory Since Plato*, ed. Hazard Adams (New York: Harcourt, 1971), ch. 9, p. 82. Roberts's translation is the one used, apparently, by Wimsatt and Beardsley. I have abbreviated Longinus's quotation from the *Iliad*, XV.605–607.

3. *On the Sublime*, ch. 9, in Adams, p. 81.

4. *An Essay on Criticism*, 675–680, in *The Twickenham Edition of the Poems of Alexander Pope*, I, ed. E. Audra and Aubrey Williams (New Haven: Yale University Press, 1961), p. 316. On the significance of this convention, see Neil Hertz, "A Reading of Longinus," in *The End of the Line: Essays on Psychoanalysis and the Sublime* (New York: Columbia University Press, 1985), p. 1.

5. Edward Young, *Complete Works*, ed. James Nichols, 2 vols. (1854; rpt. Hildesheim, Ger.: Georg Olms Verlagsbuchhandlung, 1968), II, 563–564. The passage quoted also appears in the excerpt from Young's *Conjectures* in Adams, *Critical Theory*, p. 345.

6. *The Poems of John Milton*, ed. John Carey and Alastair Fowler (London: Longman, 1968), p. 640.

7. In leading her away from her image, the voice is of course also saving Eve from the fate of Narcissus, who was destined to die when he came to recognize that the image in the water was merely his own reflection (Ovid, *Metamorphoses*, III.339–348, 463–503).

8. I use the unattractive compound "Platonic/Socratic" for two reasons: first, to indicate that I take no position on the traditional question of how far Socrates, as Plato constructs his views, stands for the views of Plato himself; second, to avoid confusion with the larger Platonic tradition, which is frequently more sympathetic to poetry than is Plato's Socrates.

9. Quotations of Plato are from Benjamin Jowett, trans., *The Dialogues of Plato*, 4th ed., 4 vols. (Oxford: Clarendon, 1953); *Ion* is in vol. 1, *The Republic* in vol. 2. Parenthetical transliterations of *Ion* are based on the Greek text in the Loeb Classical Library's *Plato in Twelve Volumes*, 8 (Cambridge, Mass.: Harvard University Press, 1925).

10. The phrase "mimetic contagion" inevitably recalls the work of René Girard, though I by no means intend to invoke the full apparatus of

Girard's systematic account of mimetic violence. Among Girard's many works on this subject, see especially *Violence and the Sacred* (Baltimore: Johns Hopkins University Press, 1977).

11. *On the Sublime,* ch. 7, in Adams, p. 80.

12. For an intriguing recent attempt to base a (preliminary) theory of literature on the notion of exemplification, see Joseph F. Graham, *Onomatopoetics: Theory of Language and Literature* (Cambridge: Cambridge University Press, 1992). For commentary on the theme of exemplification in Wimsatt's writings, see the same work, pp. 229–246.

13. At the phrase "self-conscious 'infinite variety,'" an asterisk directs us to the following explanatory note: "I do not mean that self-consciousness is the only principle of complexity in character, yet a considerable degree of it would appear to be a requisite for poetic interest."

14. Nelson Goodman, *Languages of Art: An Approach to a Theory of Symbols,* 2nd ed. (Indianapolis: Hackett, 1976), p. 59.

15. For a historical account of the traditional association of obesity, femininity, and literary excess, see Patricia Parker, *Literary Fat Ladies: Rhetoric, Gender, Property* (New York: Methuen, 1987). For an account of Falstaff in particular as a variation on the figure of the "fat lady," see pp. 20–22.

16. Cf. René Wellek and Austin Warren, *Theory of Literature,* 3rd ed. (1949; rpt. New York: Harcourt, Brace, and World, 1956), p. 249: "What the formalist wants to maintain is that the poem is not only a cause, or a potential cause, of the reader's 'poetic experience,' but a specific, highly-organized control of the reader's experience, so that the experience is most fittingly described as an experience of the poem."

17. Both these options, of course, are supposed to be equally bad from Wimsatt's official point of view, with the former corresponding to the Intentional and the latter to the Affective Fallacy.

18. For a related but somewhat different account of the connection between formalist aesthetics and the Longinian shifting of agency between author and reader, see Frances Ferguson, "A Commentary on Suzanne Guerlac's 'Longinus and the Subject of the Sublime,'" *New Literary History,* 16 (Winter 1985), 291–297. In Ferguson's intriguing formulation, "the aesthetic tradition that appropriates Longinus culminates in a dissolution of the subject in the person of the author and in a reinscription of the subject in the person of the reader, hearer, or viewer." The analysis I have been pursuing ends up somewhere closer to the received understanding of formalism. It suggests that, at least in some versions of modern formalism, the transfer of agency is for the sake not so much of shifting power from one agent to another as of collapsing the difference between concrete agency and universal meaning, thus saving literary discourse

(and, indirectly, those who produce it or read or study it) from the Platonic/Socratic charges of perverse concreteness and empty universality. In other words, the appeal to the reader's subjectivity is for the sake of idealizing the text and not the other way around. On the other hand, this chapter opened with an acknowledgment of how readily such exchanges can be reversed—which is itself part of the scandal to which an appeal to the notion of a "concrete universal" is one response.

19. I. A. Richards, *Coleridge on Imagination* (1934; 3rd ed. Bloomington: Indiana University Press, 1960), pp. 82–83; Richards is quoting *Coleridge's Shakespearean Criticism*, ed. Thomas Middleton Raysor (Cambridge, Mass.: Harvard University Press, 1930), I, 217.

20. Richards, *Coleridge,* pp. 83–84.

21. Jean-Paul Sartre, *The Psychology of Imagination* (1940; English trans. Secaucus, N.J.: Citadel, 1980), p. 35; hereafter cited in the text as *POI.*

22. I am not, of course, suggesting any specific recollection on Sartre's part of the details of Plato's texts, or any conscious concern at this point to counter the Platonic/Socratic hostility to imagination.

23. On the importance of "intensity" and "exact duration" as features of imaginative experience, see Roger Scruton, *Art and Imagination: A Study in the Philosophy of Mind,* 2nd ed. (London: Routledge and Kegan Paul, 1982), pp. 101–103.

24. See ibid., pp. 108–109, following Richard Wollheim, *Art and Its Objects* (New York: Harper and Row, 1968), secs. 11–14. For Wittgenstein's original discussion of the example, see Ludwig Wittgenstein, *Philosophical Investigations,* trans. Elizabeth Anscombe, 3rd ed. (New York: Macmillan, 1968), pt. II, sec. xi.

25. Cf. Donald Davidson, "What Metaphors Mean," in *Inquiries into Truth and Interpretation* (Oxford: Clarendon, 1984), p. 263.

26. See John R. Searle, *Intentionality: An Essay in the Philosophy of Mind* (Cambridge: Cambridge University Press, 1983), pp. 65–70.

27. Mary Warnock, *Imagination* (Berkeley and Los Angeles: University of California Press, 1976), p. 169.

28. Warnock's term, in *Imagination,* p. 170.

29. Again, on the importance of indexicality for the intentional content of perceptual experiences in general, see Searle, *Intentionality,* pp. 62–71.

30. Warnock, *Imagination,* p. 170. Without embracing his metaphysical understanding of it, I am indebted here to Nicholas Wolterstorff's notion that a fictional character is "a certain kind of person, that is, not a *person* of a certain kind but a certain *person-kind*" (*Works and Worlds of Art* [Oxford: Clarendon, 1980], p. 144). For reasons indicated later, however, I would extend this notion beyond the case of *fictional* persons.

31. The concrete universality of persons as they are perceived "in" their

bodies is complicated, however, by the fact that still another kind of concrete universality applies to persons *as agents.* I will postpone an account of this second kind of concrete universality, however, until Chapter 5 and the Conclusion.

32. The emphasis on language and culture, like the apparent hostility to affect, is an expression of Wimsatt's and Beardsley's larger project in these essays—in essence, to found the claims of literary criticism as a quasi-scientific discipline on the public status of literary meaning.

33. Ronald de Sousa, *The Rationality of Emotion* (Cambridge, Mass.: MIT Press, 1987), p. 182.

34. To say that the object-types "refer to" new scenarios is not to say that the *words* denoting these object-types acquire new meanings. The changes involved here are not necessarily *linguistic* changes.

35. My account of the effect of inserting something into a "new composite scenario" was in some respects anticipated by New Critical remarks on what happens to a statement when it is qualified by its placement in a particular poetic "context"; see, for instance, Cleanth Brooks's 1949 essay "Irony as a Principle of Structure," rpt. in *Critical Theory since Plato,* ed. Hazard Adams (New York: Harcourt Brace Jovanovich, 1971), pp. 1041–1048. See also Murray Krieger's extended treatment of what he calls "the contextual theory," in *The New Apologists for Poetry* (Minneapolis: University of Minneapolis Press, 1956), passim. Nowadays in literary criticism, of course, the term "context" is almost always used to denote the external circumstances of a text's production or reception *in contrast* to the interrelation of elements within the literary artifact itself. Terminology aside, however, it seems to me that the irreducible interplay of typicality and particularity suggested by Wimsatt's theory of the "concrete universal" gets closer to the actual source of literary fascination than does the more casual organicism informing Brooks's treatment of contextual "irony."

4. Literary Value

1. Compare Louise Rosenblatt's still-plausible summary of the benefits of literary study for adolescents, in *Literature as Exploration* (1938; 4th ed. New York: Modern Language Association, 1983), pp. 222–223.

2. Ronald de Sousa, *The Rationality of Emotion* (Cambridge, Mass.: MIT Press, 1987); hereafter abbreviated as *RE.*

3. *RE,* pp. 184, 343n3, citing Iris Murdoch, *The Sovereignty of the Good* (London: Routledge, 1970), and Martha Nussbaum, " 'Finely Aware and Richly Responsible': Moral Attention and the Moral Task of Literature," *Journal of Philosophy,* 82 (October 1985), 516–529. The second item appears, revised and expanded, in *Literature and the Question of Philosophy,*

ed. Anthony J. Cascardi (Baltimore: Johns Hopkins University Press, 1987), pp. 169–191.

4. Donald Davidson, *Essays on Actions and Events* (Oxford: Clarendon, 1980), p. 41. As de Sousa notes, his "principle of emotive continence" is directly modeled on this Davidsonian "principle of continence."

5. Throughout what follows I will be using the term "liberal" not in the narrow sense current in contemporary debate but to refer to the broad range of ethical and political theories and values associated, since the late seventeenth century, with Anglo-American and European modes of representative government. For a systematic analysis of "liberalism"—as well as a defense of the notion that it *can* be analyzed systematically—see Roberto Mangabeira Unger, *Knowledge and Politics* (New York: Free Press, 1975).

6. Hanna Fenichel Pitkin, *The Concept of Representation* (Berkeley and Los Angeles: University of California Press, 1967), ch. 4.

7. Ibid., p. 63, citing John Stuart Mill, *Utilitarianism, Liberty, and Representative Government,* Everyman's ed. (London: J. M. Dent and Sons, 1947), pp. 239–240. Catherine Gallagher, however, has explored Mill's own skepticism toward the descriptive theory suggested by passages like this one; see *The Industrial Reformation of English Fiction: 1832–1867* (Chicago: University of Chicago Press, 1985), pp. 229–233.

8. Pitkin, *Concept of Representation,* pp. 63, 90.

9. Ibid., p. 63, quoting Mill, *Utilitarianism,* p. 239.

10. Derek Attridge, *Peculiar Language: Literature as Difference from the Renaissance to James Joyce* (Ithaca, N.Y.: Cornell University Press, 1988), p. 15n4, quoting Paul de Man, *The Resistance to Theory* (Minneapolis: University of Minnesota Press, 1986), p. 11.

11. Paul de Man, "The Purloined Ribbon," *Glyph,* 1 (1977), 28–49; hereafter abbreviated as "PR."

12. De Man bases this possibility on an ingenious reading of Rousseau's statement, "Je m'excusai sur le premier objet que s'offrit" ("PR," p. 36; cf. p. 40).

13. Steven Knapp and Walter Benn Michaels, "Against Theory," *Critical Inquiry,* 8 (Summer 1982), 733–736.

14. For the record of de Man's activities, and a sample of the debate occasioned by their discovery, see Paul de Man, *Wartime Journalism: 1939–1943,* ed. Werner Hamacher, Neil Hertz, and Thomas Keenan (Lincoln: University of Nebraska Press, 1989), and the companion volume (same editors, press, and date), *Responses: On Paul de Man's Wartime Journalism.* In her contribution to *Responses,* Catherine Gallagher discusses the use of de Man's "Purloined Ribbon" essay by various parties to the debate (p. 206).

15. According to de Man, the "random error" that presents itself as Rousseau's speech act reveals that "there can be no use of language which is

not . . . radically formal, i.e. mechanical, no matter how deeply this aspect may be concealed by aesthetic, formalistic delusions" ("PR," pp. 41, 42).

16. Chinua Achebe, *Things Fall Apart* (New York: Fawcett, 1959).

17. Ibid., pp. 133, 137, 140–141, 145–146.

18. A graduate student of my acquaintance once argued on those grounds that it was a bad idea to teach Achebe's novel.

19. Bernard Williams, *Ethics and the Limits of Philosophy* (Cambridge, Mass.: Harvard University Press, 1985), p. 51.

20. The last point is forcefully argued by Bernard Williams in his discussion of Plato's Callicles; see *Ethics,* ch. 2.

21. Richard Rorty, *Contingency, Irony, and Solidarity* (Cambridge: Cambridge University Press, 1989).

22. A preference for "thick description" over principle is an important theme of Rorty's book; see for instance *Contingency,* p. 94. The phrase itself, of course, derives from Clifford Geertz.

23. John Locke, *An Essay Concerning Human Understanding,* ed. Peter H. Nidditch (Oxford: Clarendon, 1975), p. 263 (book II, ch. XXI, sec. 47); emphases in original.

24. The quoted phrases, repeated from earlier chapters, are, respectively, from *The Letters of John Keats,* ed. Hyder Edward Rollins, 2 vols. (Cambridge, Mass.: Harvard University Press, 1958), I, 193; and William K. Wimsatt, Jr., *The Verbal Icon: Studies in the Meaning of Poetry* (Lexington: University Press of Kentucky, 1954), p. 273.

25. In associating the literary "concrete universal" with the fundamental structure of the liberal conception of agency and not with a potential alternative to it, my account differs, for instance, from Unger's; see *Knowledge and Politics,* pp. 137–144, 224–226.

26. A convenient introduction to this movement, or at least to the current debates about its identity and value, is H. Aram Veeser, ed., *The New Historicism* (New York: Routledge, 1989). The recent tendency I refer to here is by no means the first attempt of literary scholarship, since the New Criticism, to move "beyond formalism" (to use a phrase of Geoffrey Hartman's that goes back several decades). There are in fact numerous forms of historicist and materialist criticism that do not take the particular form I have in mind, namely, the form of making a work's social context itself an object of *literary* interest in the special sense I have been developing.

5. Collective Memory and the Actual Past

1. An earlier version of this chapter appeared in *Representations,* 26 (Spring 1989), 123–149.

2. The precise manner in which a canonical narrative serves to authorize particular proposals can be extremely subtle and varied, as is amply shown, for example, by David H. Kelsey in *The Uses of Scripture in Recent Theology* (Philadelphia: Fortress, 1975).

3. On the post-Enlightenment interaction between theology and historical criticism, see Van A. Harvey, *The Historian and the Believer: The Morality of Historical Knowledge and Christian Belief* (Philadelphia: Westminster, 1966) and Hans W. Frei, *The Eclipse of Biblical Narrative: A Study in Eighteenth and Nineteenth Century Hermeneutics* (New Haven: Yale University Press, 1974); for an overview of the most recent phase of this history, see Norman K. Gottwald, *The Hebrew Bible: A Socio-Literary Introduction* (Philadelphia: Fortress, 1985), pp. 16–20.

4. Gerhard von Rad, *Genesis: A Commentary,* trans. John H. Marks, rev. ed. (Philadelphia: Westminster, 1972), p. 19n.

5. Maryknoll, N.Y.: Orbis, 1979; and New York: Crossroad, 1983. These works will henceforth be cited in the text as *TY* and *MH,* respectively. For a recent, fascinating, but for present purposes too complex version of the reconstructive tendency, see John Dominic Crossan, *The Historical Jesus: The Life of a Mediterranean Jewish Peasant* (San Francisco: Harper, 1991).

6. George E. Mendenhall, "The Hebrew Conquest of Palestine," *The Biblical Archaeologist,* 25 (1962), pp. 66–87.

7. In observing that Gottwald and Schüssler Fiorenza have in one sense merely shifted the locus of scriptural authority, I am not implying that the authority they confer on the biblical events is necessarily the same in kind or degree as the authority more orthodox interpreters impute to the biblical texts. Schüssler Fiorenza, for instance, rejects the notion that the "counter-voices and visions" she uncovers constitute a "norm to be obeyed" or a "canon to be observed"; their value lies instead in their capacity "to give liberating vision, courage, hope in liberation struggles today" (*Protocol of the Colloquy of the Center for Hermeneutical Studies in Hellenistic and Modern Culture,* 53 [1987], 54). In that case, my question is still why it should matter that such benefits derive from the (actual) past.

8. "The Theological Task after *The Tribes of Yahweh,*" in *The Bible and Liberation: Political and Social Hermeneutics,* ed. Norman K. Gottwald (Maryknoll, N.Y.: Orbis, 1983), p. 198.

9. Readers familiar with structuralist terminology will notice a resemblance between my use of the terms "analogy" and "causality" and the structuralist habit of contrasting "metaphor" and "metonymy." This suggests that there may be a connection between tendencies to essentialize the actual past and a certain structuralist manner of idealizing literary lan-

guage (that is, by privileging figures in which metaphoric and metonymic relations happen to coincide). But I will not pursue this
suggestion any further in the present context.

10. *American Slavery—American Freedom: The Ordeal of Colonial Virginia* (New
York: Norton, 1975), ch. 18.

11. *The Political Unconscious: Narrative as a Socially Symbolic Act* (Ithaca, N.Y.:
Cornell University Press, 1981), p. 17; henceforth cited in the text as
PU.

12. The mode of analysis in the remainder of this chapter requires frequent
reference to a generic "agent." Rather than use repeatedly a hybrid pro-
noun form that the reader would rightly find distracting, I will henceforth adopt the convention (unsatisfactory, of course) of switching,
periodically, between feminine and masculine.

13. To ask whether personal and collective pasts have similar claims on the
present is not to imply any endorsement of a philosophical or an ethical
or political individualism. I am in no sense questioning the view that
persons are socially constructed—that, in the words of George H. Mead,
"The self, as that which can be an object to itself, is essentially a social
structure, and it arises in social experience" (*Mind, Self, and Society: From
the Standpoint of a Social Behaviorist,* ed. Charles W. Morris [Chicago: University of Chicago Press, 1934], p. 140). Nor am I questioning the
numerous other ways, apart from relations to the past, in which personal
and collective identities can be treated as homologous. For a discussion of
such homologies, see Jürgen Habermas, *Communication and the Evolution of
Society,* trans. Thomas McCarthy (Boston: Beacon Press, 1979), pp. 106–
116. Finally, to conclude that agents are *not* accountable for their collective pasts would not be to absolve them of collective responsibility for
their collective presents and futures.

14. For a recent critical survey of theories of punishment, see C. L. Ten,
Crime, Guilt, and Punishment: A Philosophical Introduction (Oxford: Clarendon, 1987). Important earlier studies include H. L. A. Hart, *Punishment and Responsibility: Essays in the Philosophy of Law* (New York: Oxford
University Press, 1968), and George P. Fletcher, *Rethinking Criminal Law*
(Boston: Little, Brown, 1978). As a glance at any of these works will
show, my argument addresses only a very narrow range of the questions
associated with what is in fact a bewilderingly complex subject.

15. "As the National Socialists well knew in controlling inmates in slave
labor camps, occasionally hanging an innocent person effectively deters
disobedience by other inmates" (Fletcher, *Rethinking Criminal Law,*
p. 415).

16. Of course even deterrence would collapse if more than a few people knew
about the deception.

17. *Philosophical Explanations* (Cambridge, Mass.: Harvard University Press, 1981), p. 387.

18. Stronger, for one thing, than the theory of personal identity Nozick himself advances in the first chapter of the same book.

19. The precise relevance of metaphysical debates about free will and determinism to theories of punishment is unclear in any case. See Derek Parfit, *Reasons and Persons* (Oxford: Clarendon, 1984), pp. 323–326.

20. In a lucid chapter on collective responsibility, Joel Feinberg distinguishes between vicarious liability and vicarious guilt. According to Feinberg, "even though criminal liability can transfer or extend vicariously from a guilty to an innocent party, it cannot literally be true that guilt transfers as well. For guilt to transfer literally, action and intention too must transfer literally. But to say of an innocent man that he bears another's guilt is to say that he had one (innocent) intention and yet another (guilty) one, a claim which on analysis turns out to be contradictory" (*Doing and Deserving: Essays in the Theory of Responsibility* [Princeton: Princeton University Press, 1970], p. 232). The question I am asking here is whether it makes any more sense to transfer action and intention from past to present states of a single person than it does to transfer them from one person to another. If not, then all guilt, not just some cases of collective guilt, is "vicarious."

21. As this sentence indicates, I am not advancing a skeptical or reductive account of personal identity as such. My claim is not that temporal succession deprives the agent of any continuous identity; it is instead the narrower suggestion that time has removed the past act from the agent's present control, and that this makes it hard to see why responses to the agent that would have been justified while she was performing the bad action remain justified *after* she has performed it.

22. This account of what is logically involved in distinguishing a particular agent from the type of agent he or she exemplifies might, if elaborated further, provide the Miltonist in Chapter 1 with a theory of personal identity that could answer the Romantic Argument. It also reveals a surprisingly close connection between the problem of our relation to the actual past and the notion of the "concrete universal" discussed in Chapter 3. For more on that connection, see the Conclusion.

23. There is, however, no guarantee that any actual practice of punishment will in fact cause people to avoid certain actions because of the effects those actions will have on their future relation to themselves. There is, in other words, no reason to suppose that a practice of punishment understood along these lines would not be futile; and if it did succeed, it might do so for the wrong reasons, perhaps by inducing a state of fear

that would have little to do with people's actually believing themselves potentially *guilty.*

24. On the crucial role of anticipation in a person's relation to her own identity, see the penetrating critical survey of German and Anglo-American theories of identity in Wolfhart Pannenberg, *Anthropology in Theological Perspective,* trans. Matthew J. O'Connell (Philadelphia: Westminster, 1985), ch. 5.

25. As George P. Fletcher observes of consequentialist theories generally, all of the "predicted goods" of punishment "are highly speculative" (*Rethinking Criminal Law,* p. 414).

26. I am indebted for this line of reasoning to a conversation with Bernard Williams.

27. *After Virtue: A Study in Moral Theory,* 2nd ed. (Notre Dame: University of Notre Dame Press, 1984), pp. 220–221.

28. My own view, strictly beside the point here, is that "affirmative action" and similar policies designed to compensate for the effects of slavery are sufficiently justified precisely by the existence of *ongoing* injuries and *present* inequities, though I have no doubt that public awareness of the past makes such phenomena somewhat harder to ignore than they would be if slavery were simply forgotten.

29. See, for instance, John A. T. Robinson, *The Body: A Study in Pauline Theology* (Philadelphia: Westminster, 1952). Even in these cases, however, there are often grounds for skepticism about the degree to which the assertion of collective singularity is to be taken literally. An insistent use of bodily images might show, as Robinson argues, that Paul conceived of the church as "a specific personal organism" (p. 51). But the frequency of Paul's recourse to such images can just as easily suggest that their purpose is not literally descriptive but allegorical and hortatory. When, in a passage like 1 Corinthians 12, relations among church members are compared to relations among specific bodily organs (foot, ear, eye, hand, genitals), this impression becomes overwhelming.

30. Such ethical values would be in some respects analogous to "natural kinds" as analyzed by Saul A. Kripke; see *Naming and Necessity* (Cambridge, Mass.: Harvard University Press, 1980), pp. 116–144.

31. Morgan himself, for one, does not appear to think that the connection was necessary; see *American Slavery,* p. 381.

Conclusion

1. W. K. Wimsatt, Jr., *The Verbal Icon: Studies in the Meaning of Poetry* (Lexington: University Press of Kentucky, 1954), p. 273; discussed earlier in Chapter 3.

2. On the formalism implicit in the self's relation to its objects, viewed from the perspective of Kantian aesthetics, see Frances Ferguson, *Solitude and the Sublime: Romanticism and the Aesthetics of Individuation* (New York: Routledge, 1992).

3. For more on the logic of practical self-conceptions, see Philip Clayton and Steven Knapp, "Ethics and Rationality," *American Philosophical Quarterly*, 30 (April 1993), 151–161.

4. This point is related to the Romantic Arguer's attack, in Chapter 1, on Milton's theory of agency, although the broader account of agency I am developing here, like the analysis in Chapter 5, actually has a tendency to work in Milton's favor. It suggests that the logic of agency as such may require that an agent be connected with her past in something close to the way the Romantic Arguer denied was coherent.

Index